THE GARDEN LETTERS

Elspeth Bradbury

&

Judy Maddocks

The Garden Letters

◆

Elspeth Bradbury & Judy Maddocks

Judy Maddocks
+
Elspeth Bradbury.

POLESTAR
BOOK PUBLISHERS

Published by:
Polestar Press Ltd.
1011 Commercial Drive, Second Floor
Vancouver, BC   Canada   V5L 3X1

The publisher would like to thank the Canada Council, the British Columbia Ministry of Small Business, Tourism and Culture, and the Department of Canadian Heritage for their ongoing financial assistance.

Interior design by Jim Brennan
Cover design by Jim Brennan.
Elspeth Bradbury photograph by Robert Bradbury.
Judy Maddocks photograph by Tom Maddocks.
Editing by Suzanne Bastedo.
Printed in Canada by Best Book Manufacturers.

Canadian Cataloguing in Publication Data

Bradbury, Elspeth.
        The garden letters
ISBN 1-896095-06-2
1. Bradbury, Elspeth—Correspondence. 2. Maddocks, Judy—Correspondence. 3. Gardeners—New Brunswick—Correspondence. 4. Gardeners—British Columbia—Correspondence. 5. Gardening—New Brunswick 6. Gardening—British Columbia. I. Maddocks, Judy. II. Title.
SB451.36C23B7 1995   635'.0971   C95-910425-9

for Tom

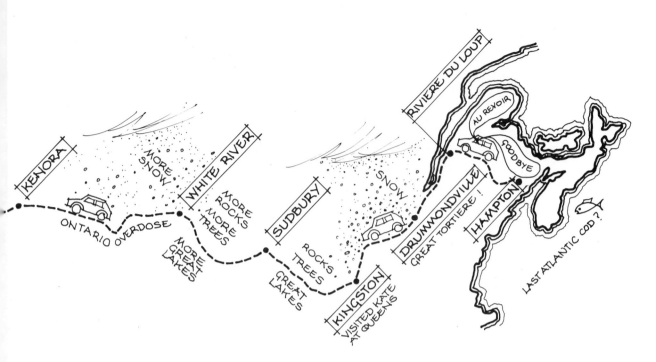

 Vancouver, British Columbia
February 4

DEAR JUDY,
The weather couldn't have been worse. For us, it couldn't
have been better. By the time we left, the snow had turned
to freezing rain and I didn't even look back for a last glimpse
of the garden. What garden? We simply slid down the
driveway, out of the past and into the future.

It took us ten days coast to coast. Quebec was snowy,
Ontario vast, and the prairies numb with cold but
unexpectedly beautiful. It was all pleasantly uneventful until
shortly after Calgary, when things took a dramatic turn.
Everything happened at once: tremendous claps of thunder,
lightning, rainbows, sunlight streaming through purple storm
clouds and, to cap it all, the car radio, which had been on the

blink since we left New Brunswick, crackled into life and the uplifting strains of Rachmaninoff's Piano Concerto no. 2 swept us into the Rockies as if we were heroes in an epic movie. Pretty special effects for anyone, and heady stuff for an anxious, middle-aged couple crammed into a small car with credit cards, clothes and computer!

We hadn't expected the future to be glorious — only warmer. We felt suddenly daring, suddenly magnificent. We WERE magnificent. Of course it didn't last, but even brake failure on Rogers Pass couldn't dampen our spirits by then and we slithered all the way to the Pacific in low gear and a state of reckless euphoria.

We sped straight through Vancouver and only the big green buffer of Stanley Park stopped us from plunging headlong into the ocean. Green Stanley Park. Green trees, green grass, and — forgive me for this — it's true about the daffodils.

Rob and Kimi had found us a downtown apartment and provided the essentials: frying pan, mattress and a fine Boston fern. We're on the fourth floor, with a narrow balcony and a sideways view of the sea. It's a treat to have a dishwasher, though we don't have many dishes, and apart from dusting the Venetian blinds, there isn't much to do in the way of chores. There's certainly no snow to shovel, no woodstoves to stoke, no hens, ducks or ponies to feed. Ray started temporary work with a firm of architects this week. I'm finding out about employment possibilities with landscape architects.

It's exciting to see such a range of unfamiliar trees and shrubs growing around the city but it's also humiliating to find myself so suddenly ignorant. The broad-leaved evergreens are the biggest challenge: *Rhododendron,*

Escallonia, Skimmia, Pieris...

I've been making good use of the library and have been to some nurseries. VanDusen Botanical Gardens will be a godsend and I'm hoping to visit the University of British Columbia gardens soon. I walk round the streets examining everything with leaves. People probably think I'm a little odd but nobody bothers. That's one of the wonderful things about Vancouver's West End — odd is not unusual. Another wonder is the quantity of flowers: tulips, irises, lilies, potted primulas and pansies, hyacinths and orchids, stacked up on staging outside the convenience stores and supermarkets. I'm told they stay there, out on the sidewalks, most of the winter.

I feel as if I'm on holiday. In spite of the Boston fern and the primulas (I couldn't resist) the apartment isn't really home yet and never will be. We've lived too long too close to the ground to change into fourth-floor dwellers now. An off-white carpet in the hallway doesn't smack of real life. I never thought I'd say this, but I miss the mud. I certainly miss the farm and all our friends. Ray needs a house to knock into shape and I need — well, you know what I need — a garden. So, this weekend, we begin the search. Ray will be looking for a promising house with a small piece of land. I'll be looking for a promising piece of land with a small house.

We have another, very happy reason for wanting a place of our own, and soon. We're going to be in-laws. Rob and Kimi have announced their engagement and are planning to be

9

married, here in Vancouver, at the end of May. We'd love to have the ceremony at home, and I'm trying not to panic at the prospect of organising a wedding in the midst of beginning a whole new life.

Hard to believe we left New Brunswick only two or three weeks ago. It's exciting to be starting from scratch at our age but, oh dear, I didn't know it would be so hard without you all. I'm finding that I didn't slip out of the past as neatly as I thought; shreds of it are clinging all over me. I'm still not sure what made us do this. Some kind of middle-aged madness? After twenty winters in the Maritimes, I think in the end we couldn't face one more interminable wait for spring.

Please write soon.

Love, Elspeth

 Kennebecasis River Road
Hampton, New Brunswick
February 14

DEAR ELSPETH,
We were all worried about you and Ray going off into the wilderness, in January of all times. Secretly, I hoped you'd find it so difficult that you'd turn around and come home again. And what a welcome in the Rockies! Thought it was the Second Coming, eh?

The weather here is wretched, of course. Schools were closed for a few days because of the snow. Large knife-edged

drifts around the back door, of a pale luminous green — such a delicate colour I was loath to break through them. In fact, I was so taken, I thought I might stay in till spring.

Oh! A car has just slid into the ditch outside the house. Four high-school girls have leapt out, giggling. Two men have stopped to offer help, all laughing and talking. The tires are spinning, men and girls are straining… it's out of the ditch at last, but oops, it's now deep in snow, on the lawn of the house opposite. The car pushers are wearying. I recognize one of the men as having had a triple bypass a few years ago; that makes it even more exciting. Now a man is in the driving seat — I'm holding my breath — they're pushing like crazy — it's on the road again — slewed across the centre this time, sliding a bit — but now they're off and running. Well, that's *my* excitement for the day.

No one here is fine; it's either flu, bronchitis, asthma or good old cabin fever, and just now, a fourth-floor apartment anywhere seems quite attractive.

And I don't want to hear any more about the antics of those overachieving daffodils, nor banks of flowers on the sidewalk. They remind me of my all too brief stay in California. I don't envy you looking for a house. When we moved up to New Brunswick from North Carolina (another place with a gorgeous climate), it was a chore trying to find one. But I've probably told you all about that, haven't I?

Congratulations to Rob and Kimi and good luck with the house hunting.

This is a short letter because I'm saving my strength to dig out the car in the driveway — that's if I can find it.

Love, Judy

Vancouver, B.C.
March 7

DEAR JUDY,
So good to get your letter!

We have great news. In a week, Ray will be flying back to New Brunswick to tackle the mammoth task of sorting, chucking out and packing our belongings. And I'll be moving into our new house.

It all happened more quickly than we dared to hope. We'd been spending every spare minute driving round with a realtor and I'd even begun to understand the local real estate jargon: handyman special (leans and leaks), cute rancher (concrete floors and a window box), peekaboo view (if you stand on the roof you can see the ocean).

We had an appointment to look at a house in Horseshoe Bay and there was some delay so the realtor suggested a cup of coffee. "Or," he said, "you could glance at a property that came on the listings last night. It has an English garden." We glanced. English garden may mean anything from a curved path to a few perennials, so we weren't expecting anything special. The house, in fact, didn't look like anything special, but the area was lovely, with a forest park across the road, and the place did feel like a home. It didn't take us long to realise it felt like *our* home. For Ray, the large room on the ground floor was the clincher; the realtor called it a bedroom but it looked, to us, suspiciously like our future office.

The next day, we put in an offer, were accepted, and I've been walking on air ever since.

The garden — how can I describe the garden — a jungle? A joke? A joy? It isn't English or any other nationality, but it is special; it must contain one of every plant known to horticulture, and possibly a few besides.

The house sprawls down the west side of the lot, so the garden is in three parts: front, back and the narrower piece in the middle. I'm still a bit hazy about the details. My impression of the front is a short driveway sloping down from the road, with an ugly rock wall on the left and, on the right, a jumble of trees and shrubs including some sort of weeping monstrosity that looks like a bird's nest coming unravelled. A ratty-looking cedar hedge runs along the road. The middle portion of the garden, beside the house, is mostly filled with a pond, but it's so overgrown we didn't even notice the water until our second visit. The back falls away from the house to a boggy dell. No lawn. Apart from a large outcropping of rock, the whole thing is solid plants and almost impenetrable. You think I'm exaggerating?

On our last visit I remember seeing, in a space no bigger than your kitchen, three deodar cedars, a corkscrew hazel, a small Douglas fir, a maple, several wild cherries and a tame plum (I knew it was a tame plum because it still wore its faded nursery tag). Assorted shrubs were crowded underneath and, at the bottom of the heap, were yuccas, sword ferns and a sprouting mat of leaves, which looked horribly like ground elder. More unidentified leaves may have been *Crocosmia*, a plant I haven't seen since I left Scotland twenty-five years ago.

Somebody obviously loved the place at one time, somebody with eclectic taste and a collector's passion. I have a picture of her in my head (I'm sure it's a she). She's pushing her way through the tangle with a few seedlings balanced on the tip of a trowel. She's searching for

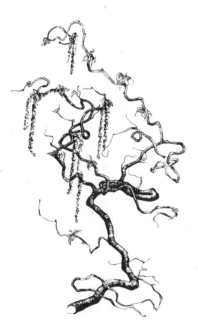

Corkscrew Hazel
Corylus avellana
'Contorta'

13

something. Ah — there — a tiny patch of bare earth! Tenderly she plants a baby horse chestnut and goes on her way well pleased, her eyes glued to the ground. If she looked up, she might notice that her treasure has landed directly under the branches of an apple tree, which is under a white pine, which is a few feet from a hemlock. Her husband meanwhile is trying, as instructed, to wedge a young golden clematis between a firethorn, an ivy and a climbing rose. "It's no good," he calls to her. "There's no more room."

That's why they left. I'm sure of it.

We've had three gardens in our day and, like yours, they've all been started pretty much from scratch. I always thought it would be fun to inherit a garden ready-made. Well, this one will be fun all right — and a lifetime's work to sort out and turn into ours.

I can hardly wait to get going, but it'll be hard finding time in the next few months because I'll have my hands full with the wedding plans, to say nothing of my new job, which starts just after I move into the house. I'll be working with a firm of landscape architects in the city. I'm looking forward to working with other people after being a one-woman practice for so long, but I'm worried that all my hard-earned knowledge about winter hardy plants and frost-proof construction methods will be useless here.

Which brings me back to winter in New Brunswick and the beautiful snow drift round your back door. It reminded me of the kitchen door at the farm. Remember? It was glass panelled and we put it in one summer. That winter, the storms came thick and fast with hardly a thaw between and soon, instead of looking into the garden, we were looking at a cross section of a huge drift. We could see the layers of crystals building up like strata in sedimentary rock or annual rings in wood, and by the end of February we could read the door as if it were a history of the winter. A gentle light filtered through it, and gazing into the snow's soft underbelly I could understand how plants can nestle in duck down comfort while freezing rain and wind wreak havoc overhead.

So, take heart! I hate to think of you still locked in winter but your garden is probably doing just fine.

I never heard how you came to buy your place. First thing I knew, a family had moved in, with British accents and two boys in school with Jean, Rob and Kate. If I'd known at the time you were fresh from Carolina, I'd have rushed round with firewood and woolly sweaters. That windy hilltop must have come as quite a shock.

Love, Elspeth

 Kennebecasis River Road
Hampton, N.B.
March 19

DEAR ELSPETH,
I thought I'd told you about how we came to buy this house. It was an experience, I can tell you. There seemed to be nothing around at the time. One day, Tom and I, Jonathan and David — they were in elementary school then — were driving aimlessly around, and saw a house standing in a windswept field with a broken FOR SALE sign swinging in the breeze. Along the front of the house was a line of tall elms,

and across a field a magnificent view of hills, a river and marshland. The sun was just filtering through the clouds and the water flowing between islands of grasses and rushes was like navy blue velvet flecked with gold. I was seduced by the view when I should have been paying more attention to the two-and-a-half-storey farm house clad in aluminum siding and an old barn frantically trying to hold on in the wind.

I remember us all peering in through the windows; the house was empty so we tried the front door and walked in. Do you know the saying, "There's a fine line between rustic and ramshackle"? Well that's what came to my mind and actually has never quite left.

The house had been divided into two apartments, a cobbled-up job that hid an extraordinary curved mahogany banister and a collapsing moulded ceiling. There was plenty of space. The boys ran wild, upstairs into the attics, and downstairs into the basement. Layers of linoleum and old carpet covered the floors and the kitchen hadn't had a paint job since it was built. The kitchen ceiling was sagging from the weight of the bath upstairs, but outside the window, across a piece of ground wild with burdock and horseradish, was a rock face that gave the back yard a lot of privacy.

No garden of course, just an overgrown field with tall clumps of lilac, the elms, a few large maples and a mock orange. The rock was covered with lichens and mosses from a pale powdery green to a green as deep as a forest. This too was flecked with gold. I was again seduced by the view when I should have been paying more attention to the plumbing.

We bought the house, and along with it we bought work! As you know, it has sucked up money like a sponge. We asked a carpenter's advice on how to re-do the hall, put in insulation and plaster board and repair the moulding. He told us we must "molest" the windows and door frames. Ever hear that term? I'd never come across it before nor since. He meant that we should take off the pine trim from around the windows and doors. After we'd "molested" we found the date when the house was built written in pencil along a beam — June 1860. Alas, the rock I spoke of was not on our property, and some years later it was smashed to smithereens because it was in the path of a builder. We should be able to save natural beauty such as this, through some enabling legislation that allows us to take out Preservation Orders. As is often the case in selling old farms, the land is sold for subdivisions and the house is left on about an acre of ground. But it's the ground that's given me a lot of joy. I can't remember when I really started the garden because we were overwhelmed with the house — still are. The pity is I didn't know you when we first moved in; you could have saved me a lot of mistakes.

Since "gardening is of the summer months" and it will be a while before *we* have summer months, I was just sitting here in the kitchen reading your letter again. I'm intrigued by the jungle. Would you like me to send a machete? I wonder which is easier, inheriting a garden ready-made, or starting from scratch? Which gives more satisfaction?

I can't imagine what I was thinking about when I started the one I have now. I started on the front lawn with a small round isolated bed that was soon scuttled by wind, children and soccer balls. I knew nothing about soil and position and what survives in this climate. I remember growing portulaca, half-hearted portulaca; I've never grown it since.

In the years after we bought the house, it was the era of ditches, deep, wide and long ditches dug across the property at random I thought, but no, there was a plan — drainage and sewage. We went from cesspool to village sewage in one fell swoop. The mess! One large boulder was left in front of the back door and we had to clamber over it to get into the house. Smaller rocks and earth were strewn everywhere. Around the house, the ground was beaten down and looked terrible but I didn't know what to do about it, so went to the beach instead.

For some reason I brought home bags of largish pebbles — egg-shaped ones, pearl coloured ones, flat pink-and-white ones — and tipped them onto the beaten ground. I had in mind to make a flower border along the wall by the back door, and use the pebbles as an edge like a little path. I didn't know you very well at the time, and you came by with a cutting of your honeysuckle. You asked me what I was doing and mentioned that I might have trouble keeping the weeds out of the pebbles. I have trouble keeping the weeds out of *everything*. But we discussed what I had in mind for the whole entrance area. I wanted to make a path up to the back door and edge the path with old bricks I'd found, then put shrubs on one side and a small border on the other. In the curve of the path I thought I'd have a small grassed area.

First I collared the boys to roll the stone from the door (sounds biblical), then I shaped a path out of the bricks. I got really excited about this and kept at it until dark.

During the night, I had a brain wave as to where I could get the gravel for the path. From the sides of the road! I didn't want to be seen scavenging, so I got up, found a bucket and went out. There, to my joy, where the two roads intersect, was a pile of loose gravel. I scooped it up into the bucket but couldn't move it — it weighed a ton — so tipped half of it out. This was going to be a long process, this path. After a while I became quite bold. The gravel, I told myself, will only be pushed into the ditch during the winter plowing, so why not make use of it? Next time I took the wheelbarrow with me. I couldn't budge *it* either. As Edna St. Vincent Millay said, "It's not true that life is one damn thing after another — it's one damn thing over and over."

One evening after dark I was out with my wheelbarrow scooping up gravel, when suddenly a light flashed on and a voice said, "Lady, d'you have a permit for that?" I thought I'd end up in jail smashing rocks. I looked up and saw to my relief a neighbour out for a walk. We laughed and he helped me push my barrow home.

You don't know how thrilled I was when, in bed one night, I heard the first crunching sound of footsteps on the gravel; it made me feel I had a real path at last. I'm so easily pleased!

Even now I can't resist gravel at the side of the road. Whenever I see a pile of it I jump out of the car and fill up my plastic bag.

Shortly after I'd been collecting gravel for the path I was in the post office getting a neighbour's mail from her box. I looked up and there stood Palmer. Did you ever know Palmer? He does odd jobs and always badly. His time is generally taken up with his health.

Without thinking I say, "How are you, Palmer?" Palmer always tells you how he is and he is never well. I'm caught between the rows of boxes, I look for escape routes, but short of leaping over him I'm stuck.

"You know I've been in the hospital," he says to me. "Had another operation."

"Oh, Palmer," I say, not in sympathy, but in bored anticipation of another trip through Palmer's vital organs.

"Yes," he says. "It made me feel I was twenty again."

I perk right up. "Really, Palmer," I say, suddenly interested.

"D'you know," he says, "I was passing stones and gravel."

Oh Palmer, you're the man for me!

Love, Judy

 Water Lane
West Vancouver, B.C.
April 2

DEAR JUDY,
Your long letter was like a life line. I've been living in the empty house for almost three weeks with only the computer, frying pan, Boston fern and primulas for company. Even Palmer would be a welcome addition right now.

I loved your description of the gravel-gathering, and I know exactly what you mean about the satisfying crunch. Have you noticed how many gravel paths and driveways find their way into the sound tracks of British movies?

Ray has probably been to see you already but I know he's working flat out at the farm, trying to get everything packed up or sold. However hard I find my new job, I wouldn't change places with him. Winding up the loose ends of twenty happy years is no fun. I'm learning the joys of commuting, faxing and filling out forms, and I've also learned I'm not cut out for any of them. Yesterday, I faxed a drawing of a fence to a local firm of architects. I thought I did. A few minutes later, the drawing came back (from somewhere in the States) with a line of washing drawn on the fence and the scribbled comment NICE FENCE. WHY? The firm I'm with does mostly large-scale jobs and I'm more comfortable working with private gardens than with contracts for impersonal landscape installations around condominiums and commercial buildings. The staff are all half my age and twice as confident. They are also wonderfully patient and parental with me as I blunder through the jungle of office procedures.

Believe it or not, I've done nothing in our own garden — another jungle. True, it's been raining pretty steadily and I don't have much time or energy left after work, but these aren't the real reasons for my idleness. I'm in shock.

Whenever I go outside, I discover four or five new plants. Sometimes the plant is a treasure — a rooted cutting of a tiny evergreen azalea, sometimes it's shoots of an invasive demon — morning glory, horsetail, bramble. I've also discovered the West Coast slug. The first one I saw was oozing across the narrow path behind the house and I nearly stepped on it. Ooooff! It was longer than my hand, thicker than my thumb and a sickly yellow blotched with brown. I've come across plenty of them since, ranging in colour from putty to jet black, but they still stop me dead in my tracks.

I keep noticing plants in danger of being throttled — or of throttling — and they're usually things I don't recognise. If I don't know what they are, how can I know how big they grow, what conditions they like? How can I decide if I should leave them, shift them or get rid of them? Where could I put them anyway? I simply don't know where to begin.

Everything's growing like crazy and it's a scrum out there. A wisteria has lassoed a white pine. A rowan is choking a holly. A walnut is locked in combat with a Japanese angelica — and seems to have won. It's a free-for-all but, in a way, splendid. The whole thing has reached that romantic stage of disarray that comes before the outbreak of total anarchy and I'm tempted to say, "What a lark, what a jolly crowd, what the heck!" It's depressing to know that whatever I do will make things look worse before they can begin to look better.

We think of plant communities as peaceful. They're not, of course. They're battlefields which seem calm only because the skirmishes are fought in silence and slow motion, often underground. A garden is just a lull in the warfare, a lull which exists only as long as the gardener's authority lasts. We're the arbiters, the little gods. Tough job.

Frankly, it's too tough for me right now. I'm just not feeling up to it. Even the simplest thing, like getting a B.C. driver's licence, seems impossible. Driving anywhere is hell. First time I tried to drive home from work, I was swept all the way round Stanley Park. Let's face it, I'm a hayseed! The hardest part is that you are all thousands of kilometres away. I don't have freezing rain here but I don't have friends either, only Rob and Kimi. (I've hardly had a chance to think about the wedding and I'm starting to panic.) I keep hoping we'll persuade Kate to move west but she loves the Maritimes. Jean is a better bet. I watch people chatting and laughing, on buses and in restaurants, and I'm so envious I could cry. I do!

Sorry to sound so miserable. I suppose the excitement of the move was bound to give way, sooner or later, to the bleak realities of being an outsider in a strange place.

Love to all, Elspeth

 Kennebecasis River Road
Hampton, N.B.
April 12

DEAR ELSPETH,
You do seem down in the dumps. Who was it who said, "When I'm down in the dumps I always get a hat"? To which her acquaintance replied: "I often wondered where you got them." I think it was Mrs. Patrick Campbell.

But I have just the thing to cheer you up. It's part of an old gardening column I found in the strangest place.

There's been a move afoot in this household to build me a garden shed, though I don't know what I've done to deserve it. It's to be where the old outhouse stands or rather stood at the bottom of the garden. I have never asked for a garden shed as there always seemed enough room in the garage/workshop for any number of tools, but it will be nice to give them a room of their own.

So today we tore down the old outhouse. Fortunately Jonathan and David were home for a spell before starting their summer jobs. I was sorry to see the outhouse come down. I'd woven all sorts of stories about its original users; I pictured one of the men in there worrying about his wife

23

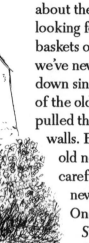

who was in labour or one of their children being sick or about the farm, if they could afford a new tractor and looking for one in the catalogue. One time I even hung baskets of geraniums from the window and door. Fortunately we've never had to use it. It didn't take much effort to tear it down since most of the wood was rotten. I think the weight of the old square nails kept it anchored to the ground. We pulled the roof off in a couple of minutes then attacked the walls. Between the shingles and the boards I found some old newspapers! After looking at the first one I was more careful in separating board from shingle. The newspapers were brown and wrinkled and dated 1891. One of them was called the *Family Herald and Weekly Star* and cost one dollar a year. Imagine them lasting that long and still being readable.

After finding the papers I took a break and went into the house. I needed a magnifying glass to look at some of the pieces. Skimming over them I came across part of a gardening column written by a man I'm sure we would both love. He spoke of visiting a friend's garden. I've copied it out for you:

> … *carnation poppies, some very large, some quite small, some round and neat, some full and ragged like Japanese chrysanthemums, but all of such beautiful shades of red, rose, crimson, pink, pale blush, and white, that if they had but smelt like carnations instead of smelling like laudanum when you have the toothache, they would have been quite perfect. In one way they are nicer than carnations. They have such lots of seed, and it is so easy to get.*

I asked John to let me have some of the heads. He could not possibly want them all, for each head has enough in it to sow two or three yards of a border. He said I might have what seeds I liked, if I used scissors, and did not drag things out of the ground by pulling. But I was not to let the young gentleman go seed gathering. "Boys be so destructive," John said. After a time, however, I persuaded him to let Harry transplant seedlings of the things that sow themselves… Harry got a lot of things for our Paradise in this way; indeed he would not have got much otherwise, except wildflowers; and, as he said, "How can I be your Honest Rootgatherer if I mayn't gather anything up by the roots?"

Isn't it beautiful? Can't you see them in John's garden on a warm hazy summer day, chatting away, admiring a large perennial border alive with hollyhocks, delphiniums and poppies? The writer of the piece probably has string tied around the legs of his pants and most likely has string in every pocket. I wonder if Harry the Honest Rootgatherer is his son? They talk about "our Paradise." Then in comes the villain of the piece:

A day or two before, the Scotch Gardener had brought Saxon to see us, and a new kind of mouldiness that had got into his grape vines to show John.

He was very cross with Saxon for walking on my garden. (And I am sure I quite forgave him, for I am so fond of him, and he knew no better, poor

25

dear!) But, though he kicked Saxon, the Scotch Gardener was kind to us. He told us the reason our gardens do not do so well as the big garden, and my Jules Margottin has not such big roses as John's Jules Margottin, is because we have never renewed the soil. Arthur and Harry got very much excited about this. They made the Scotch Gardener tell them what good soil ought to be made of, and the rest of the day they talked of nothing but compost.

At first I thought Saxon was a person who didn't know any better than to walk on the garden. It was only when the Scotch Gardener gave him a kick that I gathered Saxon was a dog. D'you suppose Saxon was the Scotch Gardener's dog? If so, you'd think he'd know better! I can hear him criticizing the 'Jules Margottin' roses: "Look at that measly little flower, and the white fly! You call yourself a gardener!" They say you can decompose almost anything in a good hot pile, so maybe, just maybe, they tipped the Scotch Gardener onto the compost pile, with Jules Margottin egging them on. I wonder if the 'Jules Margottin' rose is around anywhere nowadays?

Wouldn't the Honest Rootgatherer love your jungle garden? Think of all the thinning he could do. All pulled up by the roots and you wouldn't notice they'd gone. It would be another paradise to him.

I must go back to clearing up the outhouse debris and hauling it to the dump or else the Scotch Gardener will be breathing down my neck.

Love, Judy

Water Lane
West Vancouver, B.C.
May 6

D<small>EAR</small> J<small>UDY</small>,
Your letter arrived the same day as Moses the cat and I was
badly in need of both. Almost immediately, things began to
pick up. Ray called to say he'd be back in a few days, Kathy
Hooper called to tell me she was coming to visit on her way
to Oregon, the rain stopped, I learned to drive home without
circumnavigating Stanley Park, and I even drove all the way
out to the airport without any mishaps.

   Did you ever see Laidlaw's cat? Their daughter flew it to
New Brunswick from the West Coast, and the poor thing was
in such a state it fled into the basement of its new home and
refused to come out for two years. I had misgivings about
having Moses shipped as freight. I thought it might be
kinder to leave him at the farm where he'd already used up
most of his lives, but in the end we decided it would be
kinder — to me — to bring him here. I was a nervous wreck
when I went to fetch him; I thought the signs I was following
read AIR FRIGHT. But I should have known better than to
worry. Moses is one cool cat. He took the journey in his
stride and even his travelling blanket (my old cableknit
sweater) recovered after a good wash.

   I kept him indoors for a few days, but now he seems at
home in his new territory. Unfortunately, while this house
was empty, the neighbourhood cats had carved up the
garden between them, and Moses, who never shied away
from a scrap, is busy renegotiating the frontiers. It would be
interesting to see a map of cat territories laid over a map of

people properties; I wonder if any of the boundaries would coincide? Anyway, Moses' tooth-and-claw negotiations have already cost me one wildly expensive trip to the vet, and I sincerely hope that peace will break out soon.

Apart from his territorial disputes, it's great to have him here. Whenever I venture outside, he's there, eager to show me around, parading in front of me, or lying in ambush among the rhododendrons. And as always, he's good for a laugh. His first encounter with goldfish (the pond, to my delight, is stocked) was a comic gem: desire at one end, dry land at the other, and Moses growing longer and longer in the middle. Anyway, thanks to him, the place already seems less foreign.

You were right about the old newspaper column; I loved it — once I'd sorted out who was who. The only literature we found in our two-seater outhouse at the farm was an ancient girlie calendar hanging on a nail. It was still there, years after we turned the place into a hen house. I could never tell if the hens approved. John and the Honest Rootgatherer not only cheered me up but slowed me down for a few minutes while I enjoyed their stroll among the opium poppies. I've been busy.

Our pared-down belongings have arrived at last. The furniture is a bit sparse but we're desperately trying to make the house look presentable before the wedding. It's to take place in the morning with a party in the afternoon. There was talk of holding the ceremony in the park, on the rocks overlooking the sea — a lovely romantic idea, but the possibility of rain and the thought of everybody scrambling around dripping wet, in their best clothes and with dainty shoes on slippery rocks, was too awful to contemplate. Both

Jean and Kate are flying west for the occasion, my father will be over from Britain, and Kimi's parents are coming from Japan. They've never been abroad before so the trip to Canada will be a great adventure for them. For us too.

As you can imagine, the garden is taking a back seat, but there is progress. Having Kathy here for a few days made all the difference. I told her I didn't know where to begin so she said, "Why not the front?" and grabbed a pick axe, then set about a mass of weedy St. John's wort growing between the road and the cedar hedge. Her energy was so infectious I finally put spade to earth myself. Pretty gravelly earth it was too and not an earthworm in sight. The result at this point is a muddy mess — not exactly the image I'd like to present to the wedding guests — but at least I now have A PLAN. I'm going to start at the front and work my way to the back. The rules are:

1.   Stick strictly to THE PLAN.
2.   Buy no new plants.
3.   Start composting (the Scotch gardener would be proud of me. By the way, I don't think he's as big a bully as you think. I'm not too keen on dogs in my garden either).

This place really is a horticultural zoo. I began to count the number of trees we have but after forty species I gave up. I have no idea how many there are all told. Pushing my way through the brambles, I feel like one of the great plant hunters. What will I come upon today — a valuable umbrella pine? A white trillium under a magnolia or a rose in a thicket of raspberries? Another iris? A blue spruce? Yesterday it was a hawthorn, not some seedling upstart but a respectable specimen. It must have been standing there, perfectly visible, all along.

Umbrella Pine
Sciadopitys verticillata

We simply can't see the trees for the trees and I know we'll have to get rid of some. I don't know how we'll ever decide which ones, but at least it shouldn't be hard to choose between the walnut and the Japanese angelica. The English walnut is an aristocrat and even its name, *Juglans regia*, means regal walnut. The angelica, on the other hand, is a bit of a weed and has a reputation for throwing up fiendishly prickly suckers. Gardening books damn it with faint praise. You know the kind of thing I mean: *A useful plant if all else fails*, or *A good tree for out of the way corners*. Ours isn't out of the way; it's about a metre from the walnut and right up against the edge of the deck. Its branches jut out at odd angles and stop abruptly as if they'd shed their twigs in the throes of a dire disease. To be honest, I thought it was dying. I was wrong. It has suddenly erupted into fountains of coppery growth. It's easier to admit my mistake since I read that Roy Lancaster was once fooled as well. (Roy Lancaster is one of my heroes, a highly respected English plantsman.) He was an apprentice when he cut down a leafless angelica, and the head gardener boxed his ears. Good thing I'm the head gardener here.

My ignorance is laughable. So many of the shrubs, especially the broad-leaved evergreens, are new to me. Of course I know my way round mugo pines, spireas and all the other ironclad hardies, and I'm getting a grip on laurels and viburnums but among shrubs such as *Sarcococcas*, *Osmanthus* and *Leucothoes* I'm still at sea. As for the vast rhododendron tribe...

At the farm I had a couple of 'P.J.M.' rhododendrons (dear old recognisable 'P.J.M.') and one or two unnamed plants which were hybridised by a local rhododendron enthusiast,

Dr. Brueckner, who moved to Ontario where he patiently continued his pursuit of hardiness. They were kept, like endangered animals, in that small enclosure we had by the greenhouse.

Growing up in Britain during the war — I'm sure you remember — most municipal parks and large gardens were overgrown with neglected laurel and rhododendrons. From a child's eye view they were huge, dark and dank, and the big purple blobs of flowers seemed as ominous as thunderclouds. In eastern Canada the tables were turned; I felt sorry for the rhododendrons. They looked so sparse and vulnerable in winter with their drooping leaves rolled up more tightly than brandy snaps.

Now I'll have to get my relationship with rhododendrons on a better footing because this garden is ideal for them and, as you can imagine, the previous owners took full advantage of their good fortune. (By the way, I was right about the gardener-in-chief being female. A neighbour told me the couple have now moved to the land of your birth, Wales. Good choice! There are still some bare hillsides there — at least there were.)

It hardly seems right for a rhodo-illiterate like me to be entrusted with this eclectic bunch: minuscule ground huggers, leggy giants, scraggy cuttings, and domes of purple, pink, yellow, red and orange blooms with foliage that ranges from the big tough leaves of 'Anna Rose Whitney' to the small soft foliage of *R. augustinii* and the tiny appendages of *R. impeditum*, which don't even come close to my concept of rhododendron.

You will realise from these names that I am, however, making an effort. On one of my early list-making strolls I remember mentally checking off the rhododendrons I considered junk. Five or six miserable runts. Three nameless rooted cuttings. 'President Roosevelt' with sickly looking variegation. Two great spindly things with scruffy leaves dangling down.

But what was this? These two had strange trunks, smooth and cinnamon coloured, and where the bark split there was a silky chartreuse underskin. Rhododendrons? I blush to think of it. I'm so green I didn't even know an arbutus when I saw one.

The *Arbutus menziesii* is the only broad-leaved evergreen tree native to Canada, and hereabouts it's the tree that everyone who's anyone knows and loves. It's fondly called the madrona. You can curse a cedar if you care to, you can even despise a dogwood, but you don't dare mock a madrona. I've seen a few symmetrical, free-standing specimens but, for the most part, they are wildly eccentric, leaning and wandering as the spirit moves them. In dry situations, the trunk bulges at the base as if it's melting.

They hate to be transplanted and resent any attempt to pamper them with good food or a decent supply of water. Lucky the gardener with established trees! A certain status goes with them, comparable to that of antique family furniture and old money. I confess I didn't think much of them at first but it hasn't taken me long to learn that the funny-looking non-rhododendrons with the touchable skin are two of my most precious possessions.

I'm feeling much better about the garden because I now realise I've been doing exactly the right thing — not much! It's impossible to grasp, in a few weeks, how this piece of land with its outrageous assembly of plants could ever relate to us — how the sun and wind move across it, how the water drains through it, what its moods are through the seasons. I don't know how long it will take me but someday — this year, next year? — I'll get going and, in the meantime, I'll keep cursing the rush hour on Lions Gate bridge, and trying to make friends with the office fax.

It's high time I stopped thinking about the garden and started thinking about food for the wedding party. I'm going to make things like sausage rolls and lemon tarts (when?) and we'll order trays of sushi so the food will be half British, half Japanese. A good B.C. mix. I'm trying to keep calm but I wake up at night in a sweat wondering WHY ME? and WHERE CAN I RENT CHAMPAGNE GLASSES? and WHAT AM I GOING TO WEAR? and WHAT ABOUT LUNCH? and HOW CAN I EXPLAIN TO KIMI'S PARENTS THAT A MUDHOLE ISN'T REALLY MY IDEA OF A FRONT GARDEN? I'm taking a few days off work but I really need a few weeks — and a few friends to help me — alas!

Wish you were here. I mean it!

Elspeth

 Kennebecasis River Road
Hampton, N.B.
May 17

DEAR ELSPETH,
You do seem to have jumped right into the middle of life again. Organizing a wedding would about finish me off! How

is your Japanese? Or will it be all bowing and gesturing? A new job, a new daughter-in-law, a new house, a new garden, and I am having a new garden shed. So things are looking up for both of us.

And the shed is coming on a treat. I'm thrilled out of my mind. After we'd torn down the outhouse a neighbour came with his small back hoe and pushed earth and large stones out of the way and flattened the ground for the timbers to rest on. There were some massive stones to be moved because the outhouse was next to a long-gone pig sty.

I think we destroyed the tall coneflowers that hugged the outhouse like a buttery ruff; I feel badly about that. I don't know how I'd cope with your jungle. I'd never have the heart to get rid of anything. Just now I have a pine and a maple, both are almost a metre high, growing right beside each other. And I can't decide which one has to go... I think I'll leave it to them. So how you can ever decide between two mature trees is beyond me.

Anyway, the frame is up. The boys and Tom have been working on it quite amicably; I see them laughing and throwing the hammer at each other. Amicably throwing the hammer!

It's to be two-and-a-half by three metres and the window on the south side will extend out like a small greenhouse so that I can put seedlings in there. The "greenhouse" will protrude about half a metre and we'll use old panes of glass for it.

They've built the floor first. Next they'll construct the walls on it and tip them up into position. It's to have a gambrel roof so they tell me. Pretty fancy! Anyway, they are getting on with it and have called for beer.

A few days later:

(It sounds like a play.) The gambrel roof is up and Jonathan is hammering the shingles on. It does look very nice I must say. The outside is board and batten. When the windows are in position, I think I'll stain it a sort of reddish brown. I am also having a bench — no, not for sitting — a bench/shelf to put things on — and racks for spades and rakes.

I can't wait to get all my tools in there and hung up. There is room for the lawn mower and a pair of broken-down garden chairs, the folding sort, the only bits of garden furniture I possess.

Why is it I've never managed to amass any garden furniture? In other people's gardens, we are invited to sit down and have a drink; in mine, we have to perch on a wall, or now, I suppose, we can lean against the garden shed. If I had garden furniture I'd then have to have a deck and if a deck then a barbecue and I once had a barbecue. It was when we lived in Texas. I was always hearing my neighbours yelling: "Throw a couple steaks on the barbecue, Jerome," and I thought I could do the same, so I got a barbecue. It took forever to get the coals hot. It was August, and the temperature was way up there, as you'd expect in Texas. Sweat poured off me. Tried: "Throw a couple steaks on the barbecue, Tom," but it didn't work, so I threw them on myself. A large dog appeared out of the blue, jumped up and ran off with the meat. Never barbecued again.

I feel now I should have garden furniture to go with the garden shed. I'd like a stone bench to put by the lilac hedge and a couple of wooden chairs under the lindens and a low, round wooden table, where I could have a cup of tea in the "dappled shade." I don't care for Adirondack chairs. I think

they have an air of melancholy about them. Tom says he's never seen anyone sitting in them and that they are always in pairs, perched on lawns, facing commanding views. I saw one at the side of the road the other day; it looked as though it had fallen off a truck. No one was sitting in it either.

The bench I covet is one you see in English gardens, a carved back with intricate latticework painted white. I've never been keen on metal furniture. I think of catching one's behind in the metal laths of the chairs. Often you see ornate metal chairs on either side of a door, but there is no feeling of comfort about them.

Is a hammock considered garden furniture? I don't want to encourage sloth and I've seen too many cartoon movies that use hammocks as props for slapstick — fat people struggling to get in or out.

And what about a sundial? Is a sundial garden furniture? I wouldn't mind one with Hilaire Belloc's verse carved around the edge:

I am a sundial, and I make a botch
Of something done far better by a watch.

Much later:
The garden shed really looks lovely, with a coat of stain that went on quite easily. I'll paint around the windows with white. The mower is in there, and the spade and fork and all manner of tools are hanging up and looking very much at home, and I stand in the doorway and look out onto the garden. And am well pleased.

Love, Judy

Water Lane
West Vancouver, B.C.
June 15

DEAR JUDY,
Sorry it's taken me so long to reply. As you can imagine it's
been pretty hectic around here. The wedding, in spite of all
my worries, was lovely. Kimi looked exquisite in her kimono
and the ceremony was calm, thoughtful and very moving.
The weather wasn't great but good enough for photographs
outside so there was plenty of posing on the deck. I will say
this for the Japanese angelica tree: its huge new leaves made
a stunning backdrop, much more elegant than the walnut's
conventional efforts.

Kimi's parents don't speak much English and our Japanese
consists of little more than *sayonara* and *Fujiyama*, so you
can imagine how much polite gesturing and smiling went on.
Ray wrote a short speech and Kimi translated it into
Japanese for him to read aloud. Japanese spoken in a
Lancashire accent must have come as a bit of a shock but it
was received with great good humour. Mrs. Kiyoi is jolly and
outgoing, and completely demolished all our stereotyped
images of Japanese women. They live in an apartment and
Mr. Kiyoi has a collection of bonsai. Our chaotic garden
seemed to puzzle him. He wandered through it quietly by
himself looking as if he couldn't believe his eyes. I know how
he felt! Having Kimi in our family is going to add a whole
unexpected dimension to our lives.

After everything quieted down, I had time to think about
the garden again. THE PLAN is working. The front is taking
shape.

I think I already told you about the cedar hedge along the roadside and the weeping elm that looked like a bird's nest. When the elm leafed out, it looked more like a large green wig. The hedge bumped into one side of it and a trellis ran, at right angles, into the other. The planting between the two included staghorn sumacs, prostrate junipers, spotted aucubas, a Chinese fir and a purple plum. Quite an assortment!

Plants that look like things, umbrellas, corkscrews, skyrockets, are always popular at garden centres but they make me feel uncomfortable. I didn't think the wig was in the best of taste. And it wasn't only an embarrassing oddity, it was shedding leaves as if it had terminal dandruff.

I was eyeing the freak with murder in my heart when one of my new neighbours came by.

"Lovely little tree, isn't it?" she said.

I hoped she meant the purple plum, but no, her eyes were fixed firmly on the elm.

"We're all so fond of it around here," she crooned. "It's quite the local landmark."

So that was that. You don't make friends by axing the neighbourhood's favourite tree.

If I couldn't get rid of the thing, at least I could tidy it up. I combed out as much dead wood as possible and trimmed the dangling tresses, trying not to chop them off in pudding basin style. The tree seemed to appreciate its new hairdo. I had the impression it shook itself out and shaped up, but as *it* began to look better, the hedge and trellis began to look worse. A few weeks ago, in a fit of disgust, and with some energetic help from Rob and a friend from the office, we ripped them out.

39

Immediately, to my surprise, the elm started to attract attention. Cars slowed down, drivers leaned out to take a closer look and ask, "What kind of a tree do you call that?" At first I'd mumble apologetically, "I think it's just a sort of elm," but then I found myself saying, "It's a special type of weeping elm," in the tone of voice dog owners use to tell you that the hearth rug on the leash is a rare pedigree from Tibet. Soon I was adding, "It's a Camperdown, grafted you know."

I'd done a little more research on its origins. I wonder if you've ever heard the story. A gardener at Camperdown House in Scotland discovered a peculiar seedling of Scotch elm which, instead of rearing up to join its lofty parents, had taken to sneaking about on the ground. The enterprising man lopped the top off an ordinary elm sapling and grafted a piece of the seedling in its place. This happened almost two hundred years ago and cuttings from the original have now found their way all over the world.

When I learned that my elm was a Scot — a fellow expatriate — I began to take a more friendly interest in it. This is not to say I liked it, not yet. But thinking back to March, I remembered there had been a rare Vancouver snowfall; the kind of snow that comes down in large damp flakes and puts gnome caps on fence posts. It had buried the assorted shrubs and changed the tree into a sort of abstract fantasy. Not bad. In April, the whole thing had been sprigged with tiny tufts of apple green, and in May, robins had built their nest in the top knot. Maybe, just maybe, this tree was not freakish, but full of character. Maybe, if one viewed it as a living sculpture...

A sculpture should be properly displayed. There should be

space around it and a fitting base. It dawned on me that all the other plants should go. A circular driveway, I realized, would turn our rare and interesting tree into a striking centrepiece. A carpet of evergreen groundcover would lie at its feet, decorated with only a few flowers — white narcissus, perhaps?

So that's what we've been doing, and I'm ready to admit I've seen the light. I'm a Camperdown convert. The Chinese fir was a prickly pain to get rid of but the shrubs popped out with astonishing ease and when I leaned on the purple plum it simply fell over. Hard to believe, but the whole area had been planted in a shallow layer of soil laid over the remains of — an old circular driveway. No wonder everything looked sick.

Soon, I hope, we'll tackle the bank at the other side. I'm going to get rid of the rocks, regrade it to a gentle slope and plant it with shrub roses to take advantage of one of the sunny spots in an otherwise shady garden.

I'm so pleased you like your new shed. Are you planning to start some perennials in the greenhouse window right away? If you don't have time now, you could always sow seeds in the fall and keep them there all winter. The repeated freeze/thaw often helps tricky seeds to germinate. The important thing is not to let the soil go into the winter in a sodden state.

I have a favourite sundial motto too, though it isn't funny:

> *'Tis always morning*
> *somewhere in the world.*

Or how about this?

Life's but a shadow,
Man's but dust;
This diall says
Dy all we must.

Too depressing! Here's a better one:

Shadow and sun — so too our lives are made
Yet think how great the sun, how small the shade.

I found these in an old book, *In Praise of Gardens,* that Jean gave me. The pages have gold edges and the pictures of extravagant Victorian gardens have tissue paper covers. I always feel as if I should be handling it with kid gloves.
Congratulations to all the shed builders!

Elspeth

 Kennebecasis River Road
Hampton, N.B.
June 25

DEAR ELSPETH,
How exciting to have new projects to work on. I'd hardly be able to sleep nights for thinking about it. Especially all that abundance. But I wouldn't know what to do with it and I certainly wouldn't have the nerve to tear stuff out even though I think a surfeit of plants has it over a dearth any day.

I imagine I would just stare and stare at the wonder of it all. I have a clear picture of Mr. Kiyoi strolling around the garden with a very puzzled look on his face.

How you could ever leave the garden you had in Hampton is beyond me, I always loved going out there. Kath, Sophie and I wonder if we can keep up the high standards. And who shall we ask for advice and who will give us all those plants? You know, we do feel abandoned!

Isn't it a Camperdown elm growing in the Crowley's garden? The trunk is quite short and tilted a bit. It looks lovely in spring with daffodils growing beneath it; in winter, covered with snow, its shape reminds me of a giant mushroom. You are not going to believe this, but when we began losing our elms to Dutch elm disease, I thought that Crowley's odd-looking tree was an elm, and that when ours were cut down, if I left enough trunk, they too would sprout from the top and grow into a tree like theirs. Apparently, their elm looked quite sickly a few years ago and a nursery man suggested they seal the top with cement, which they did. It looks great now.

Everyone was away at the weekend, so I thought this is my *big* chance. You remember the valuable lawn ornament — you probably mistook it for a giant hair-roller — that has stood on our lawn for years? I mean the large roll of reinforcing mesh left over after the new concrete floor was put down in the garage. Tom was always going to do something with it or sell it — people would pay good money for mesh like that — but he never did. In winter I could never move it because it froze to the ground, and in summer it was bound down by convolvulus and wild pea. I had many, many times threatened to get rid of it, but the boys wouldn't take part in any more of my covert operations so I had to wait until they were all away before I could ACT. Now it's gone! Though the manoeuvre was not without complications, of course.

You remember me telling you about a guy I know, who has a slave called Hildegard, and only plants at night, under a full moon. Well, I saw him in the bank and quickly decided I could do my business another day.

I am sneaking out of the bank hoping he won't see me, when I hear a thick accent.

"How is the garden?" he asks, following me out. We talk about mulch; it seems harmless enough.

"I collect all the trees at Christmas," he says. "And my wife, Hildegard, sits in the garage and clips the branches into small pieces."

"Does she mind doing this?" I ask.

"No," he says, spitting brown from the tobacco he chews. "And now I have all the clippings to mulch my vegetables."

I ask if Hildegard does any of the gardening.

"A woman," he says, "must never go into the garden when she's menstruating. Never go near a plant. I say to Hildegard, 'Are you menstruating, Hildegard? Out!' I have seen her go down through a row of tomatoes, just touching one plant, and in seconds, the leaves just wither away and the tomato drops dead!"

"I've never heard that," I say.

"My sister said her jade plant had died.

44

I said, 'Lottie, were you menstruating when you touched it?'
She said to mind my own business. But I can always tell.
There's an acid on a woman's finger tips," he says, holding out
his stubby hands, "that when she menstruates gets onto the
leaves and poisons the plants. You don't believe me, do you?"
he says, wagging his finger. "Well, you'll see."

He goes off and I'm left wondering if it's deeply buried in
the psyches of men that women are unclean — or dangerous? Poor Hildegard! I bet she has a rough time of it. He'd
be the sort of man to wind his wife in a roll of reinforcing
mesh and say it's for her own good. And I'd always thought
that a garden was an equal opportunity workplace.

Love, Judy

P.S. I have enclosed some photos of the garden, just in case
you forget how pretty it is here in summer.

 Water Lane
West Vancouver, B.C.
July 2

DEAR JUDY,
Aphids are devouring my poor Camperdown. Not the
ordinary greenflies that seem to exude from the tips of rose
bushes — these are blue, a cobalt blue that would be
beautiful on anything but a bunch of bugs sucking the life
out of your favourite tree. When I first noticed the curling
leaves, I thought they were diseased, but when I unrolled

45

one I discovered a webby cluster of the little pests. No use
trying to blast them with soapy water, so I began the tedious
task of handpicking.

And this is how I met my neighbour.

Most of the infected leaves were on the inner surface of
the hanging branches and, as I was working, she sauntered
over to find out what I was doing inside a tree. She quickly
proved herself the best possible neighbour — the kind who
says, "Hello, I'm Anne," and without more ado starts
handpicking blue aphids off your elm.

We spent an hour or so under the leafy dome, tugging at
branches, chatting about this and that, and dodging showers
of sticky aphid excrement. Never once did she question my
sanity, never once did she stop for a break. Hildegard
couldn't have done a better job. We stuffed the curly leaves
into large paper sacks that had contained dry cat food
(enough, I'd thought mistakenly, to feed Moses for the rest of
his lives).

What do you do with sacks full of blue aphids? You can't
put them in the compost. I rolled down the tops, stowed
them in the basement to await the next garbage collection —
and forgot about them. Last Saturday, Ray said, "There are
fruit flies in the back porch." I didn't pay much attention. I
mean, one doesn't. Next day I noticed there were indeed
small black flies in the back porch — and in the bathroom
and in the kitchen — and the day after that was Black
Monday. Clouds of tiny flies swarmed from the basement,
settled like sticky soot over the walls and drifted like black
snow against the windows. A few, heaven help me, even
made their way onto Ray's drawing board.

One female aphid can produce one hundred offspring in

one month. Someone whose arithmetic is better than mine has calculated that this can, in theory, lead to six hundred billion new aphids in a year. I believe it. Apparently they can do this without male assistance, producing females — often pregnant at the time of birth — that produce more females, and so on. Like Russian dolls. The first and only generation of males is born as the temperature drops in autumn (or basements?) and their job is to help produce fertile eggs for overwintering. I don't know how many billion flies I vacuumed up, and I didn't care which sex they were, but you can be sure I sealed that vacuum bag in plastic and delivered it in person to the garbage truck on pick-up day.

After all this fuss, the elm looks no better. I sometimes wonder why I bother…

Next day:

Your letter has just arrived. I suspect there's a story lurking in your complicated hair-roller removal manoeuvre and I certainly hope you're going to tell me about it.

Thanks for the lovely photos. They're propped up on the desk in front of me and the cane chair looks almost too inviting. I long to join you there for coffee and a chat. But I'm puzzled. I can't make out where it is.

I was fascinated to hear that old myth about menstruating women is alive and well in Hampton. Did you know it was once thought we could harm plants just by looking at them at the wrong time of the month? Even more potent death rays came from girls just beginning to menstruate. If such a girl were lead three times round a garden (presumably blind-fold to be on the safe side) any caterpillars lurking in the leaves would succumb and drop to the ground. Hmm! I wonder if it would work with aphids.

Thinking about your pictures and about why we bother to garden has put me in a ruminative mood. Do you remember the photography workshop we went to at Freeman's, years ago? Well, something must have rubbed off because, although I'm still reluctant to meddle with dials and tripods, I sometimes strike lucky and land a good shot. I don't mean good in the technical sense; I mean a picture that can lift me out of my normal cobwebby condition and set me in a more vivid moment of my life.

If you were to ask a group of gardeners, "What do you cultivate?" I suppose they'd answer "vegetables" or "roses" or "every available species of alpine." A few savvy old hands might even say "the soil." I'd be very surprised if anyone said "moments," and yet I think they may be one of our most important crops.

Moments! I know, it sounds ridiculous, but bear with me!

Why *do* we struggle on year after year? Certainly not just for exercise, or to impress the neighbours. There are probably as many reasons as there are gardeners but I'm sure one of them has to do with childhood, with memories of special times.

I remember vividly the first time I saw a kingfisher. It was no more than a quick flash of iridescent colour over dark water, but I still feel a tremor when I think of it.

Another time, I was lying on a pebble beach, looking at the horizon, and everything seemed so right I've been inclined to carry pebble amulets in my pockets ever since. You once told me you had been taken to a farm when you were small. I don't remember the details but I know there were lilacs and you were absolutely happy, and that now, the scent of lilacs is enough to take you back there.

I hope all children have these fleeting bursts of happiness. They come from feeling perfectly in tune with the world and someone (Virginia Woolf, I think) called them moments of being. They grow rarer with age and can't be forced but I think they can be encouraged. The wilderness is their natural habitat but they thrive in gardens too if conditions are right. It seems to me that one essential condition is a sort of concentrated stillness.

I'm hopeless at stillness, especially in the garden. As you know, I suffer from groundsel grab and transplanter twitch, which probably explains why uplifting moments are scattered as thinly through my life as specks of green in my trays of germinating primroses. Sometimes, however, I achieve stillness unwittingly. Once when I knelt to sniff a snowdrop and stayed on my knees transfixed by its tiny perfection. Once when I was taking a snapshot of a Japanese iris and was gripped by its calm beauty against a dazzle of water. Which brings me back to photographs, because I don't believe it was only by chance that some of my rare, great garden moments happened when I was holding a camera.

If I hadn't been taking the time to peer through a view finder, I doubt if the iris would have had the chance to pull those precious seconds into focus. Even if I'd paused long enough to stand and stare, unaided by Kodak and Minolta, would the moment have taken root in my memory? I certainly wouldn't have owned a picture that's as good as a season ticket to the show.

If I'm right about moments being my garden's most important crop, then cameras must be garden tools as essential as spades and trowels, and I should smarten up and fetch my tripod from the attic. I suppose a sketch book could come in handy as well, and your cane chair might even prove to be a pretty good tool.

Love, Elspeth

P.S. I can hardly believe the coincidence! Last night, after writing this, I started reading *Letters from a Cornish Garden*, borrowed from our local library. The author is a feisty woman called C.C. Vyvyan, who once crossed the divide from Canada into Alaska looking for wildflowers and, at the age of sixty-seven, walked six hundred kilometres along the river Rhône. (Maybe I should have called her a feisty *lady* since she was really Lady Clara Vyvyan.) She writes that special moments have been the most important influence in her life. But, she says, "Seldom could I retain that heartening sense of the whole world being my garden and never could I summon it at will. It would come and go like a shooting star." Good description! Then she goes on — and here comes the bombshell — she has discovered "an infallible means of inducing that blissful sensation." According to C.C. Vyvyan, it's simple. The trick is to sleep out under the stars.

I'm adding sleeping bag to my shortlist of essential garden equipment.

Kennebecasis River Road
Hampton, N.B.
July 9

THE GIANT HAIR-ROLLER MANOEUVRE

Getting rid of the roll of reinforcing mesh was not easy. What is? I've tried for years to get rid of it and failed. Because they were all away at the weekend I thought it was my big chance to put it out for garbage pick-up. Picture this. I'm so eager to get rid of it, I get up very early and go into the garden in my robe and slippers. The hair-roller is at the top of the driveway and I give it a little push with my foot. It rolls slowly, so I give it another push, which speeds it up no end. It speeds right out into the road, a road that is usually quiet at this time of day. But, at this precise moment, a small blue truck comes by and gives the hair-roller a glancing blow. I close my eyes, and hope for the best. I hear the truck stop. Oh God, what now!

A man in a red cap bounces out. We both stand and watch the roll of mesh spin around and around in the middle of the road. I explain to him that I'm trying to get rid of it.

He says, "I'll take it."

I say, "I'll help you."

He backs his truck up and pulls down the tail-gate. As we are lifting up the heavy hair-roller, two sheep leap right over us and take off down the field.

"Quick," he shouts and we take off after them. It's beginning to rain and I'm not dressed to catch sheep. Then he yells, "D'you have any rope?"

"Not on me," I yell back, "but I'll find some." I run up to the house, put on sheep-catching shoes and find rope suitable for same.

I run down the field, though not too fast, as I wouldn't know what to do with a sheep if I caught one. I twirl the rope in the air like a steer-wrestler and catch up with red-cap. The sheep crop the grass, but as soon as we close in on them they scamper off.

"Goddamned sheep," he shouts, hitting the ground with the rope. We are both soaking wet by now.

"Are they yours?"

"No."

I'm disinclined to ask more. He crouches low and slowly creeps up on them. I stand guard with my arms out and knees bent like I see at sheep dog trials. We do this many times until finally he ropes one of them. I lead the bleating sheep up the field, the other one follows. After many attempts we hoist the struggling animals onto the truck. It's not easy hanging onto back legs going like pistons. Once, I let my half go, but red-cap, now a shepherd of considerable experience, is quicker this time.

When Tom and the boys arrive home the first thing they say is, "Where's that roll of mesh?"

"What roll?" I say.

Love from Bo Peep

Kennebecasis River Road
Hampton, N.B.
July 11

DEAR ELSPETH,
While you're worrying about the Camperdown, d'you ever wonder what makes us garden? Why you spend hours pulling off aphids? Haven't you found that gardeners here have roots in Britain or Holland? I think it's in the genes, a piece of the "old country" trying to get out.

I work like a dog out there and really just for my own satisfaction. No one would care if I left it just as it was, like a hay field. After I leave, in one year it'll probably revert right back to a hay field. It is pretty ephemeral, is gardening. Maybe that's not such a bad thing; after all, if things don't work out one year there is *always next year* — the gardener's motto. In fact, the family would like it better if I spent less time in the garden and more time making those wretched meals we women are heir to.

What I love most about gardening is finding a new area to shape into something different. I like a job that I can think about night after night, or when I'm washing up. In the depths of winter, when I'm out on the tundra shovelling snow, I often think to myself, I can move that wall, or I can enlarge that bed.

Like my new place at the bottom of the garden, the one in the photo you like. If you stand at the back door looking east, it's in that direction. It's hidden away and I sort of stumbled on it. It was overgrown with brambles, burdock, and crab grass, so a few weeks ago I found myself clearing it and once I got started I couldn't stop. I really had no intention of doing this but I hacked my way through weeds, got scratched by brambles and eaten by blackflies. In the "interior" I came across a largish rock that had bricks laid out at the foot of it. An altar? A black mass? Not a barbecue surely? The rock is about five metres away from the new shed and further in I found a pile of old bricks. I kept on chopping away until I cleared an area bounded on one side by two old apple trees, and on another by maples and then the rock with the lilacs hanging over it.

I worked until overcome by mosquitoes. All night I thought about it and started in the next day and the next. It was such a lovely feeling, the hard work and accomplishing something I really hadn't planned on. There must be an area in the brain of gardeners, which after they've worked hard to shape a stretch of garden, secretes an enzyme that gives inordinate pleasure — sounds like a sentence out of *The Joy of Sex*!

After it was finished I really noticed the scent of apple blossom. I put the cane chair in there and, for their summer vacation, I stood pots of house plants around the base of the rock. All this I have gained.

It's now like a secret place where I can sit, but of course never do because I'm as twitchy as you in the garden. But once I sat down by mistake and realized I couldn't see any flowers from there. Ahead of me, and down to the left, was a bank that had been littered for years with great timbers from the old barn. After a lot of cajoling I got rid of them, leaving large bare spots on the bank. I can never resist a bare spot, so immediately thought *rock garden,* and that's what I'm working on now. I could go on about how I dug like a fiend and hauled in rocks, but I won't. But I have some stepping stones going up through it, edged with creeping thyme.

When I'm driving in the car in the late afternoon and I see a woman strolling around her garden, bending to examine a plant a bit more closely, I think to myself, I bet she is really enjoying herself. A neighbour of mine in Wales once said that if he wanted his wife to do something for him, he asked her when she was working in the garden. He said she was always in a good mood then.

Love, Judy

Water Lane
West Vancouver, B.C.
July 23

DEAR JUDY,
I read your sheep story to Ray and we both had a good
chuckle.

I agree that creating new places is the best part of
gardening, and it sounds as if you've been having a field day.
The secret spot sounds lovely. Every garden should have
somewhere like that — a place to retreat to. Ours doesn't yet
but I'm sure I'll find the right spot somewhere near the
pond. When I get as far as the pond. I'm still working around
the driveway.

I'm not so sure I agree about genes for gardening. Most
keen gardeners come from gardening families so it almost
seems to run in the blood, but I think it might be a germ that
infects you when you're very young, something you catch
from a parent or from anyone else who takes the time to
show a toddler how snap dragons snap, or points out that
cottage pinks smell of cloves and sorrel tastes of lemon. I
caught the germ from my grandfather.

I believe the love of plants is learned, and as with most
kinds of learning it begins with games. Remember *He loves
me, he loves me not*? I wonder how many daisies we picked
apart to that rhythm, or how many buttercups we held to our
chins to ask, *Do you like butter?* While we were playing on
those long-ago lawns, absorbed in daisy chains and dandelion
clocks, rose-petal fingernails and maple-seed helicopters, I
think the germ took hold. Mind you, with most of us, the
symptoms don't show till we have gardens of our own.

Just mentioning daisy chains has made me feel deliciously nostalgic. Do you remember how satisfying it was to make fingernail slits in those thin daisy stems and thread them together without a break? I must have turned out yards and yards of the wilting stuff but, strangely enough, I don't remember wearing it. Real lawn daisies grow here so, one day, my grandchildren (I'm an optimist) will be able to make daisy chains too. I tried with the big oxeye daisies that grow so well in New Brunswick, but it wasn't the same.

Dandelions were our favourites. Chains with the stems left long made golden crowns with green hair hanging down — pretty messy hair. I wonder how often my mother warned me, in vain I suppose, not to stain my clothes with dandelion milk. And when we puffed on the seed heads to tell the time (in some parts of the world this tells you how many children you'll have) I'm sure it never occurred to us that, along with the fairy parachutes, we were spreading aggravation for the neighbourhood gardeners.

What egoists we were! We lived in a world that seemed intended for us entirely, where every flower, every stick and stone, was a potential toy, a treasure. We played five stones or *chucks* with carefully selected pebbles and, of course, a good conker was worth almost as much as a lucky marble. We flung burrs and fired plantain guns, made pea-pod canoes, raced stick-boats under bridges and made horrible noises with squeaking grass. Did you ever tattoo the back of your hand by rubbing fine earth on the sticky imprint of a flowering currant leaf?

We kept general store with dock seed for tea, hollyhock seed for cheeses and the silvery seed pods of honesty for money. There was never a shortage of imagination.

The flower of a hollyhock, its petals reflexed, was a lady in a gown. The flower of a bleeding heart, its wings pulled gently apart, revealed a lady in a bath tub — a goggle-eyed and indignant personage! A pansy without petals became a minuscule man, and if you knew how, you could expose his tiny spindly legs.

July 24

I was so carried away with my sentimental memories last night, I could hardly drag myself to bed. You'll be glad to hear I'm back on track today, if a little sleepy.

The area I'm shaping at the moment is the circular driveway. When we carved it out, we left a wide bed for trees and shrubs to screen the pond garden. What a pleasure it is to plant right up to the edge of the paving; no need to worry about snow banks and road salt. I wish you could have been here to help me choose the planting. There is such variety available, and plenty of it right in our own back yard.

Luckily, rhododendrons and camellias transplant readily, so I've been plundering the jungle for mature specimens. Our first choice was a camellia which we rescued from under a large flowering cherry. Camellias enjoy some shade but this was in permanent gloom and the poor thing hardly flowered this spring. It stands head high, but looks smaller now it's out in the open. This isn't the best time to move camellias but if I keep it watered, I think it'll pull round.

Next time I dipped into the jungle I came up with three Vulcan rhododendrons, one with a root mass well over a metre across. I had no qualms about moving this one, at least not from the plant's point of view, but it takes team work to move such large specimens and, as you know, getting the

Bleeding Heart
Dicentra spectabilis

team assembled isn't always easy. One skill I've picked up as a gardener, however, is coercion, and after a little effort on my part, everything — Ray, Rob and the rhododendron — fell nicely into place.

Spacing plants correctly in a shrubbery is impossible, like trying to be all things to all people all the time. If it's right now, it won't be right five, or fifteen, years from now. In my own garden I tend to plant for good effect in the short term and move things around when they jostle each other. It works fine with perennials and fibrous rooted shrubs like the rhododendrons, but some plants are better left in peace. I don't mess with tap roots and I don't move large trees unless I have to. At the farm, I once had to shift a pine three metres tall. I rootpruned it first and moved it the following year. The operation was successful for the pine, but it nearly killed me.

There was room for a couple of smallish trees in the new border. Ray said he didn't mind what we had as long as one was a saucer magnolia and, after Vulcan was manhandled into place, I wasn't in any position to argue even if I'd wanted to. But let us never forget, though it's hard (harder even than remembering the botanical name of dawn redwood) that a wispy sapling in a plastic pot may really, truly, grow bigger than a bread box. Actually bigger than a house. Before I bought Ray's magnolia, I forced myself to fix the image of a mature specimen on my mind's eye and then transpose it to the chosen spot. I confess I had to cheat a little. I shrank my mental magnolia and squeaked it in under the hydro wires.

With the magnolia safely in the ground, RULE 2 (Remember RULE 2? Buy No New Plants) fell into disarray. Before it had time to recover, I rushed out and bought a few new shrubs and some of the neat evergreen ground cover that's called kinnikinnick here. I used to know it as bearberry.

I'm obviously starting to suffer from the same complaint as my predecessors — horticultural greed. For the second tree in the border I was torn between a Chinese dogwood and a Japanese snowbell and, after not much consideration, I chose both. The dogwood is planted and a cane marks the place where the snowbell will go when the current period of fiscal restraint is over. Some day, when I'm gone, someone will no doubt stand in the driveway shaking her head and muttering about the fool who planted the trees too close together.

And talking about closely planted trees, Angelica has pulled another sensational stunt. This time she's done it with flowers. Clouds of creamy fluff have quite upstaged walnut's discreet productions. Maybe the choice between them isn't going to be as simple as I thought. I was looking through a tree book recently and noticed that mature walnuts grow eighteen metres across. One day, not only the deck but the entire house will be engulfed in its shade. What's more, blister mite has raised an embarrassing rash of pimples on the regal visage.

How is the rock garden progressing? No doubt you are working far too hard and enjoying yourself enormously. I certainly hope so.

Love, Elspeth

Kennebecasis River Road
Hampton, N.B.
August 2

DEAR ELSPETH,

I've been out there staring at the perennial bed and thinking
what a lovely month July has been for flowers. Staring is
something I do a lot at this time of the year. I can't believe
anything will survive the winter, then comes summer, and we
are rewarded with all this bounty.

The blues of the delphiniums alone are enough to take
your breath away, from an indigo through to a delicate egg-
shell, then the magenta and pink phlox, and next to it, a new
one, white with a dark pink centre, then the lemon lilies like
lemon sherbet and the pale salmon lily edged with a white
ruff.

 Because I stared so long I neglected the weeding and felt
guilty for not keeping up the high standards you set. My
garden will never be neat — I like it a bit wild — but it had
gone far beyond wild and looked like hell. So I've been on
my knees weeding like a fury, and realized what a relief it
must have been when man first began walking upright!
While I was weeding around a rose bush, I thought of the
rose-petal fingernails and the nasty brown concoction called
pot pourri that we made from petals. And what a terrible
smell! Did you ever make pea shooters? I think we made
them from the hollow stems of elderberry. I have a clear
memory of one boy yelling at me, "You're going to die!" He
said the elderberry stems were poisonous. He said it with
such authority that by the end of the afternoon I had a
terrible stomach ache. I liked the earrings made from pairs

of cherries best.

But back to the weeding. First I worked around some blue flax. This is the first year for flax and what a lovely surprise. It's supposed to be a perennial, even out here. I hope it is.

The dianthus does well. I have a number of different ones. Kath gave me some seeds from her dianthus so I planted them, labelled DIANTHUS: KATH. But when they came up they were POPPY: SHIRLEY! I loosened up the soil around the dianthus. Some are a dark red and some two-toned and there is a small magenta one that must be a Maiden Pink. I was very careful around the Welsh poppy. Pale yellow and delicate, it's already finished blooming and only the ferny leaves remain. I try very hard not to pull it out in my weeding frenzy, then think that maybe I should, because each year it seems to be going further and further down the bank; I've a mind to scoop it up and put it at the top, because if it continues the way it's going, it will end up in the grass and won't stand a chance. But then the Welsh are a hardy breed.

Plants do seem to travel, though. I imagine great armies of bulbs marching underground during the winter. I can swear that I planted a columbine next to the Sweet William, but come summer, they won't be anywhere near each other.

Before I forget — I was talking to Sophie about your problem of walnut versus angelica and she said she would never cut a walnut down because she'd had fresh walnuts in Czechoslovakia and they were delicious. So you have to choose between Japan and England. And since you now have a Japanese daughter, you'd better be careful.

I have quite a bit of stonecrop choked up with crabgrass. It is difficult separating them as stonecrop breaks so easily. Getting the crabgrass out makes me feel like a surgeon cutting out a growth; very satisfying. Were you with us when we brought home some wild stonecrop off the rocks at Cape Enrage? I figured that if it could live clinging onto the rocks in such a hostile environment, it could survive in my garden. It grows in clumps, is a beautiful jade colour and not pushy. I'd never seen it for sale in any nursery and had no idea what it was, until a friend's husband came by and was surprised to see it doing so well. He thought it might be *Sedum rosea,* and said that its roots smelled faintly of roses. I gave him a clump but forgot to smell the roots.

The scent from the dianthus was quite delicious when I worked around them. Next to the dianthus is William and Mary — its mottled leaves look decorative all summer. In spring, when everything looks so ratty, I'm always amazed by this first rush of colour, the pink flowers turning to blue. I imagine it is too tough for your area.

In this same bed I have a non-flowering peony. I've had it for years and it's never flowered. I dug it up and raised the crown nearer the surface, still no flowers, so I thought a different venue might help. I read an article by a woman who said she divided and moved plants any time she chose and *never* had a failure. The Mrs. Thatcher of gardening. So I, who generally walk on shifting sands, thought I could do the same. I dug up the peony and cut it up into three and planted all three in different parts of the garden. So now I have *three* non-flowering peonies. The foliage on this one is a dark bronze colour, so if I had my wits about me I could say that I grow it just for the foliage. But I am going to be

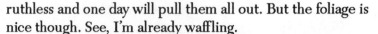

ruthless and one day will pull them all out. But the foliage is nice though. See, I'm already waffling.

The woolly thyme I got from you looks good, a comforting looking plant; I want to pat it on the head and tell it it's doing well. Next to it is a different patch of thyme. I imagine it's the common thyme. But what a lovely smell. After being on my knees for so long I wanted to stretch, so took a look at the scarlet runners. In its eagerness to get to the blossom, a ruby-throated hummingbird flew right up under my hat. And how they love the honeysuckle. I painted my toenails red one day, and a hummingbird zoomed right down at them.

There is so much ground ivy in this bed — not just this bed, but in every bed — that it drives me crazy! It has a pretty little blue flower but if only it weren't so pushy! I yank out what I can but never in a hundred years will I get it all. If only the groundhog, who now seems to have taken up residence under the new shed, was a ground-ivy-eating groundhog.

I've really been waging war on the groundhog this year, because it ate the tops of my tulips and nipped the emerging phlox. Each year I've tried to get rid of it, and each year I seem to fail. I'd heard that moth balls would do the trick so I went to the hardware store and explained why I wanted them. Jack said, "I've never heard tell of that." Anyway, I sprinkled them liberally around the shed and waited. The groundhog loved them so much I saw him and his friends juggling with them. Then I tried harassment. This meant driving a pole back and forth under the shed every half hour. It just made my arm ache and had no effect on *him*. So then

I thought of sprinkling all the old perfume I have around the garden shed. I was pretty liberal with it on the step where the groundhog likes to sun himself. Now the smell is so strong it would knock you down. I can't even go into the shed. And I still have the groundhog, though perfumed.

To go back to the weeding — when I'd finished, I gave everything a shot of fish fertilizer and promised myself a shot of gin, then I whipped around the bed with the lawn mower, ambled leisurely around the garden with my gin and tonic, and admired.

Love, Judy

P.S. Did I complain about one groundhog? I've just looked through the window and there are three small ones sitting on the wood pile.

 Water Lane
West Vancouver, B.C.
August 13

DEAR JUDY,
You're right about William and Mary; I think they really are too tough for our mild, moist climate. They mildewed here so badly this summer I was ready to yank them out, but knowing how bravely they flower at the start of the year, I couldn't do it. I've always called them soldiers and sailors. Do you know why another common name for them is lungwort? Their spotted leaves apparently look like diseased lungs and

this was thought to show their medicinal value for those particular organs. Their botanical name is *Pulmonaria* and there are several garden types including *P. angustifolia* 'Mawson's variety' which is a strong clear blue with plain green leaves. I have a soft spot for it because my first architectural job was with Mawson's firm in the north of England, and I think the variety name refers to Thomas Mawson who was a well known landscape architect in the early 1900s. He worked mostly in Britain but was involved in the plans for Stanley Park and the University of British Columbia here in Vancouver, and also prepared the city plan for Regina. His son and grandson ran the firm when I was there.

Hummingbirds still seem thrillingly exotic to me. I'll always remember the first one we saw, twenty-five years ago, after we came to Canada. It was feeding at the hollyhocks outside our window in Hampton and we were so excited we rushed to take a photograph through the glass. You can imagine how it came out — a tiny blurred dot that could just as well have been dust on the lens. At the farm I had a large clump of Cambridge Scarlet bee balm, which the hummingbirds loved. Unfortunately Moses loved it too. He learned to lie in wait among the leaves and, when the hummingbirds came to feed, he'd perform a sort of vertical lift-off and pick them out of the air. After a few heartbreaking incidents I couldn't stand it any longer and ripped the bee balm out. Moses's reflexes probably aren't as quick at this stage of his life but I'm not going to take any chances.

I know what you mean about mobile bulbs. Especially beware of lilies! You think you know where they are, so you

Lungwort
Pulmonaria saccharata

66

dig where you think they are not, and are treated to one of gardening's most stomach-turning sensations — slicing into the pure, crisp flesh of a healthy lily bulb.

I can picture your little flocks of Welsh poppies fluttering down the hill on their root tips. By the time you glance their way, of course, they are sitting at the foot of the slope, looking as innocent as only poppies can.

I find it easy to think of plants as people. Biologists throw up their hands in horror at this kind of thing. Endowing plants with human characteristics is a serious breach of scientific rules, but happily there are no unbreakable rules in gardening. If I want to call my hemlock Sherlock, by golly I'll do it.

I once had a maple called Fred who sulked, but then, he had wet feet. Jill was a yellowwood, *Cladrastis lutea*, a lovely little tree that's supposed to produce fragrant flower clusters. Jill had plenty of pluck but, in the end, the New Brunswick climate proved too much for her. Every summer she took one brave step forward and every winter she staggered two steps back until she disappeared. I always hoped I'd see her flowers cluster before she passed on, but no such luck. I've since read that yellowwoods don't usually flower until they're twenty-five years old so I'd have had a long wait in any case. If I could find the space I'd plant one here. Immediately.

To my mind, our Angelica is definitely female, maybe because she decked herself out with such flare. Alongside her exotic draperies and fluff, poor old (male) walnut was beginning to seem a bit of a bore and, what with the wedding photos and the floral display, we were thinking that Angelica might be worth saving after all. Not any longer. A snow of tiny petals has begun to filter down from her

impressive flowers and it looks as if the fallout will go on for weeks. It settles in our hair, in our drinks, on my pots of begonias and on Moses asleep in the shade. Ray has taken to eating lunch indoors. Her standing slips further every time I notice her pushy young offspring appearing in distant flowerbeds. Yesterday I pried up a paving stone and exposed a mass of writhing white roots as startling as a serpents' nest. Rumours that walnut roots exude toxins harmful to other plants are, so far, proving groundless and walnut is firmly back in favour, so you can reassure Sophie.

To get back to the poppies, I know a thing or two about these fragile-looking little toughies because this garden is full of them, both yellow and orange. Much as I love them I've decided there are limits. I've been trying to corral them in the back but it isn't easy.

They put down tap roots which recover almost as persistently as dandelions from any half-hearted attempt to weed them out, and they also seed themselves readily. Whenever I'm weeding I come across their offspring, which are like tiny parsnips. I only wish their *Meconopsis* relatives, the blue poppies, would be half as generous.

Tuberous Begonia
Begonia X tuberhybrida

The soil must be full of Welsh poppy seed because poppies reappear whenever I disturb the ground. I don't know how long the seed stays viable but such a well-distributed stock makes me think they must have been around for many years. It gives credibility to the local story about the English couple who originally settled here and laid out these winding lanes in imitation of an English village complete with church, lych gate and village green. It's said they missed the flowers of the old country and introduced seed of their favourites: foxgloves, double English daisies and Welsh poppies. We certainly have all of them in abundance. I wonder if they introduced the giant black slugs as well. Apparently these monsters aren't native, though the putty coloured ones, the banana slugs, are true British Columbians.

Did you know that mullein can sprout after seventy years? And that's nothing compared with the seeds of lamb's quarters; some were dug up in an archeological site and germinated after a seventeen-hundred-year interment. The frozen seed of the Arctic lupin has come to life after ten thousand years and I read recently that a white flower, like a magnolia, has blossomed from a seed discovered among the ruins of a two-thousand-year-old tomb in western Japan.

It's a little unnerving to think that every time you turn over the soil you may be triggering into life a whole batch of prehistoric weed seed.

Britain is full of stories about garden plants surviving long after the gardeners, and even the gardens, have been forgotten. Henbane and deadly nightshade, which were grown for herbal medicine by medieval monks, still tend to hang around old monastery sites, and the commercial daffodil growing in the Scilly Isles began with two kinds of

flowers, 'Scilly White' and 'Soleil d'Or', which were
discovered among the ruins of the abbey at Tresco. As the
Yorkshire plantsman, Reginald Farrer, said, "The immortality
of marbles and of miseries is a vain small thing compared
with the immortality of a flower that blooms and is dead by
dusk."

Even Vancouver, with its short history, has a poignant tale
of plant survivors. Off Stanley Park, there's a spit of land
called Dead Man's Island, which was occupied years ago by
squatters. Since the squatters' forced departure in the 1930s,
their garden flowers have continued to bloom every summer.
Or so the story goes. The land has been taken over by the
navy and is closed to the public but I was curious to know if
any traces really survive, so I plucked up my courage and
phoned the navy people there. I thought I'd get the brush-
off but no. They were charming and called back to tell me
that, although most of the land has been regraded, there are
shrubby roses growing near the water. Of course these could
be wild roses that have grown there forever but I'd much
rather believe they're a legacy from those early Vancouver
days.

Not much progress in the garden. My energy always seems
to flag in August. Let's hope the cooler weather in
September spurs me on to greater efforts.

You've probably noticed I'm full of information today. I've
been preparing a talk about garden history for a local club. I
gave it last night and I think it went off well in spite of an
elderly woman, dressed from top to toe in pink, who stood
up half way through the slide show (blotting out most of the
white garden at Sissinghurst).

"I 'ate gardens," she announced.

"I beg your pardon," I said, "you er..."
"'Ate 'em," she insisted. "Can't stand 'em."
"Maybe you would like to leave then?" I suggested.
But she didn't.

Love, Elspeth

Kennebecasis River Road
Hampton, N.B.
August 22

DEAR ELSPETH,
What an informative letter and interesting. As soon as I read
about Fred the beginning of a rhyme popped into my mind.
"I once had a maple called Fred, who sulked most of the day
in his bed..." Can you finish it?
  I agree, one of the worst sensations is to dig through the
unsullied flesh of a lily bulb. I look at what I've done with
horror and try to bury the whole lot as quickly as possible,
and hope it doesn't notice that it's now no longer one but
several. But on the whole I've had a lot of luck with lilies.
And am always surprised how magnificent they look, and in
my garden, too.
  I wish lavender did as well as lily bulbs. One time I had a
bush but it never did very much in spite of my covering it
with milk crates in winter, and really mollycoddling it. There
was always a lot of winter kill. It must be borderline here,
though I see it for sale in this area. Did you have a bush
when you lived here? Last year I moved it to what I thought

71

was a better place, sun and less wind, but it didn't make it through the winter, so all thoughts of sprinkling it throughout the linen closet vanished from my mind. Oh, how I fantasize. Can you imagine me ever doing that or even having a linen closet or even linen? I'll just have to do with Lavender Water — sounds so old fashioned now, doesn't it, and I can't even remember when I last had a bottle.

But in the border outside the back door, where the lavender lived, clumps and clumps of night scented stock have sprung up and the smell is just marvellous. In the evenings as I walk around the garden it drifts over me. I planted some seeds last year and didn't expect to see it again this year, but it seems better than ever. It has also taken up residence alongside the garage up through the different sized pebbles I got from the beach.

Another volunteer that looks great at this time of the year is alyssum, the purple one. It has reseeded itself along the gravel path I made. I wouldn't have thought it tough enough for the gravel path, but it seems to love it. And what a nice smell. In spring when I recognize their small beginnings I carefully dig them up and spread them along the flagstone path leading to the house. They do well there but never seem to volunteer the next year. Maybe it's because I clear the flagstone path of snow and disturb them. They also have a lot of competition from nigella and feverfew which reseed like crazy along that path. I love them both, especially nigella, though I prefer its common name, love-in-a-mist. It looks like love.

I once had a maple called Fred,
Who sulked most of the day in his bed.
He complained of wet feet and said it's not neat,
To be known as a maple called Fred.

Oh Fred, I can't get you out of my mind. Sounds like a song!

I don't know why but it suddenly struck me the other day that there is a definite right time and wrong time to look at a garden. A time when the light is the most flattering, sort of like candlelight. The middle of the night, in my garden, when you can't see the weeds!

One of the nicest times is first thing in the morning. I love to wander around with a cup of coffee when everything is fresh: the grass is damp, birds sing, and a ribbon of mist floats over the marsh. But early morning has its disadvantages; jobs crowd into my mind: I've got to get this done today, I must tie the honeysuckle back, that doesn't fit in there, and before I know it I'm digging something up.

Midday is no good at all. The shadows are all too harsh and often in summer, it's quite hot. It's always at midday that I think of watering — the worst time, of course.

The best time to see a garden is in the evening, I think, after working all day digging, watering, weeding and mowing. The shadows are long and romantic, and I feel so good about it all. The grass clipped, blossoms deadheaded and the earth around plants fluffed up. I suppose you could say I feel self-righteous, to say nothing of tired!

Once a year — I time it for an evening visit — I get Tom to come into the garden. Otherwise he would never see it, because as you know he never ventures out there. That's not strictly true because this summer he's been taking some quite lovely photographs, mostly close-ups of flowers. You'd think I had some fantastic showplace. It's not that, but I love it so much I want him to enjoy it. He asks questions like how is the shed making out and do I still like the new beautiful fork he got me for my birthday and is the lawn mower still holding up. Pointing to delphiniums, my beloved says, "I like those poppies," and wants to know the difference between an annual and a perennial, that sort of thing, but his heart is not really in it. I can't understand why someone wouldn't want to be outside all the time when the weather is good. But then I can't understand myself a lot of the time so why should I understand someone else?

Love, Judy

 Kennebecasis River Road
Hampton, N.B.
August 28

DEAR ELSPETH,
It seems, as soon as things are going well, along comes a problem that can only be solved by a ditch. Usually a Panama-size ditch that traverses most of the garden. Our problem this time is lack of water. Each summer we have been getting less and less water and the pump has been pumping for longer and longer; we are now in the process of having a new well drilled. What a performance!

The well-driller has no love for shrubbery, I can tell you. Equipment is spread all over the place: long lengths of pipe, tools galore, string and old bits of rag. He backed the truck around to the back of the house, squashing pinks, rock cress, and snow-in-summer, and came within a hair's breadth of a flowering quince. The truck is now resting about a metre away from a Grootendorst rose I got from Corn Hill Nursery a few years ago. The last time I looked it still had rosettes of red roses. I wonder if there will be anything left?

It isn't one of those fast drilling operations, but a thump, thump, thump for days on end. It's not all that efficient either; the well-driller asked me for a tape measure. He'd lost his gauge and needed to measure I can't think what, as he hasn't done anything yet. He also uses lots of safety pins that I provide. I'm waiting to be asked if I happen to have a drill.

Have just been out there to check:

What a mess! D'you suppose they know what they're doing? They've been at it now for three days. He brought his ten-year-old son to help him, a clone of the old man. Both of them are overweight with chubby red cheeks. They have identical large square teeth, with a gap between the front ones — for spitting. Neither laces up his boots of course — hope they don't trip and fall down the well, though there's little chance of that! They keep asking me for water, and I told him that was why he was here, to find it. I found out why he needed a tape measure; it was to see how tall his son was.

Each time there is a thump, the Grootendorst jumps up into the air. The irises unfortunately didn't jump high enough so got crushed, along with the tomatoes and lettuce.

Before the well-driller we had a water diviner come — my friend Palmer, a gnome of a man who walked around the garden with a bent coat hanger held in front of him. Anyway, aiming in the direction of next door's swimming pool, he told us where we would find water. He also recommended the well-driller. On his way out he noticed the rose, because, as he said, "I'm allergic to them fellahs."

Days later:

The well-drillers have gone. They were here a week, were practically part of the family. I'll probably send them birthday cards. We attached the pipes ourselves. I spent a lot of time in the basement watching a pressure gauge and yelling out when it reached the exact pressure. I got the feeling if I didn't yell at the appropriate time we'd all be blown to smithereens.

And the number of ditches left behind! One stretched alongside the house with other ditches feeding into it. A good thing about all this activity is the number of large stones that were unearthed. You know how I love large stones. I even had a plan for them.

Facing east, across from the back door, is a group of tall lilac bushes, both purple and white. The same group that shelters the "secret place." I thought I could haul the stones to the base of the lilacs and using the stones as a background, dig a curved border following the slope. I paced up and down in my rubber boots, viewing the area now thick with mud, stones and debris. I looked at it from different angles. Yes — if I could haul the stones up there I could make something of it. I couldn't wait to start.

I started raking while the ground was still muddy, so it was really hard going. I should have waited for it to dry out a bit, but you know how it is. The more I raked the more stones I unearthed. Funny how that always happens! But this time I had a home for them. I tossed them into the half-filled ditches then threw in the excess earth that still lay around. I worked for days and long into the nights doing this chore. One evening I noticed some new neighbours watching me through their window; it was better than the TV: "live from the garden."

After dispensing with the smaller stones I started on the larger ones. I had to shift some fairly big rocks. When I could, I flipped them over. I don't mean flip like in *flip a coin* — that sounds too easy. I heaved them over so they glunked their way across the ground. I had quite a struggle with some of them especially when I was pushing uphill; then I resorted to a crowbar and spade. I angled each into place at the foot of the lilac bushes, not once or twice but many many times until it was right.

When the rocks were in place I started digging. At least there was no grass to get through — the well-driller saw to that — and the digging wasn't too bad. As you know I've always loved digging; some love dancing, with me it's digging. Should have been a grave digger! After I'd had a good old dig, I added manure and compost to the soil and dug and raked again. At the bottom of the slope I found a large embedded rock; I exposed part of it and planted hen-and-chicks around it. Don't for a minute think it only took five minutes. It took forever, I can tell you. But I enjoyed it.

The fun part was deciding what to plant and where. It's a shady border because of the lilacs, though it lightened up after I clipped some back. I dug up hostas and put them with some William and Mary, then scavenged the garden for primroses and day lilies. I found wild columbine growing in a ditch, so in they went as well. I put a potted azalea on one of the stones at the back and also a jade plant. I've bought some impatiens and foxgloves.

I keep going out there to have another look and to see how I can improve it; one improvement will be to get some grass seed down, though starting lawns is not much fun. But the border makes me very happy. Had we not had the well drilled I wouldn't even have thought of it.

Love from the well-driller's friend,
who, in the turmoil, forgot to mail the other letter.

 Water Lane
West Vancouver, B.C.
September 7

DEAR JUDY,

> *There once was a maple called Fred*
> *Who sulked as he sat in his bed*
> *"I would like you to know*
> *That I simply won't grow*
> *Till you move me from this disgusting mud puddle*
>   *and address me*
> *By my correct botanical name which is* Acer
>   saccharum," *he said.*

The best time to look at this garden is after a good West Coast downpour when the sun is just breaking through heavy clouds and the light is theatrical. Then the earth steams and the air smells of leaves. The dark evergreens drip and glisten, and I can almost hear the surge of green things growing. I half wish I was short-sighted and could see it all in a romantic blur as Gertrude Jekyll and Monet saw their gardens. When I squint through half-closed eyes, the tangle of laurels and ferns, brambles and butterburs, looks wonderfully dramatic instead of alarmingly chaotic. If I could blur my thoughts as well, I might forget that the soggy undergrowth is heaven for slugs and that the task of taking all this in hand is overwhelming.

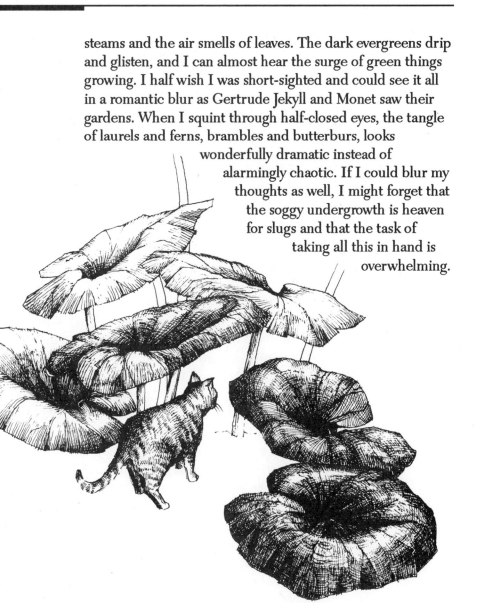

Foolish, of course, to feel I have to, but I do. I don't think I've told you about the Japanese butterburs, *Petasites japonicus*. From insignificant nubs in the spring they grew into huge round leaves. The effect was splendid at first but the leaves were soon riddled with slug holes and, when the dry weather began, they started to droop and now look as limp as dishcloths and about as attractive. Everything I've read about butterburs warns that they are horribly invasive. Help!

One of the things I like best about this property is the forest, which still stands across the road in more or less its natural state. Some of the Douglas firs and red cedars must be five hundred years old. I know it's a cliché to liken a stand of old growth forest to a cathedral, but the columns of ancient trees really do inspire reverence, and the slant of the sun through high foliage really does make me think of light streaming through lofty stained glass windows. It puts the trivia of daily life into perspective and there's no doubt it casts mere gardening into the shade. Literally in our case, because the park lies to the south.

In March, when I moved in here, I wondered if I'd ever see the noontime sun again. Happily, by May, it was rising well above the forest and, for four months, the front of the house was bathed in light. Now already, I notice the sun is starting to flicker in and out behind the tree tops again.

Does anybody nowadays still think of forests as simply a number of trees? Long ago I grasped that they were total systems of soil, plants and animals, but what I hadn't understood until we came here was that forests are also systems of weather. Under a mature forest canopy, everything — rain, wind, light, heat — is filtered and modified. Remove even one of the big trees and the light floods in while moisture rushes out like a genie escaping from a bottle.

In spring, on a day when the rain was blustering around the garden, I could walk across the narrow band of asphalt that separates us from the park, and step into another climate, where only a few drips fell to the ground and the green twigs of huckleberry barely quivered. Now, on the forest side of the road, ferns and mosses stay soft and green in the damp air and half light while, on our side, the earth bakes beside the driveway, and I drag the hose around and fret about the rhododendrons and the transplanted camellia.

Vancouver is so renowned for its rain I've been surprised to hear that summers are often warm and dry like this. Most lawns have turned yellow and, with water restrictions in force, I'm even more pleased that we have no grass to bother with. We are still allowed to water on alternate days — on dates with an even number if the street address is an even number. Soon, there may be a total ban. How we take water for granted!

More and more people are installing irrigation systems, hardly the answer in the long run. I'm going to pay more attention to plants that survive periods of summer drought. I'm glad the new planting by the driveway will function, eventually, like a forest in miniature — deciduous trees to shade the evergreen shrubs, to shade the ground covers, to shade the soil. All the same, I have done some watering. Odd evenings only of course. It's about all I have done lately and it's as much for my benefit as for the plants'. Holding a hose gives such satisfaction for such a small outlay of energy. Sometimes I can't tear myself away and Ray comes to see what I'm doing out there in the dark.

If your lavender had survived it would have enjoyed this

hot dry summer. Sharp drainage is the key. Mine did well at the farm between the stones of the patio where it grew in almost pure sand.

Love, Elspeth

P.S. Walnut has consolidated his lead; fat green nuts have appeared and it looks as if we'll have a bumper crop. We watch the gourmet nuggets swell and marvel that we ever harboured thoughts of *Juglans* regicide.

Kennebecasis River Road
Hampton, N.B.
September 18

DEAR ELSPETH,
This last couple of days, the weather has been perfect — clear blue skies with just a touch of fall. I picked enough for three vases of flowers: black-eyed-Susan, bachelor's buttons, daisies, love-in-a-mist, dahlias, bee balm and feverfew. While I was enjoying myself picking flowers, I noticed a car slowing down with two familiar faces inside. Palmer and wife! He probably wanted to see how his well-drilling friend made out. Palmer's wife has one topic of conversation: "When I went into labour… " and it's always terrible and the doctor's never seen anything like it. I've never liked listening to women going on about their labour — I bet Palmer's had labour pains — so I instinctively flung myself down among the bee balm and put my hand on a bee. So now I have a red swollen itchy hand to remind me how nasty I was — I used

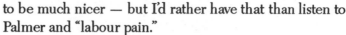

to be much nicer — but I'd rather have that than listen to Palmer and "labour pain."

It's been pretty dry here, but Vancouver having to restrict the use of water seems bizarre. Need a new well? How about a water diviner? Sophie was very envious of you having walnuts and said she doesn't know how you can ever *think* of getting rid of a walnut tree. She's relieved you're not going to.

I've also been gathering seeds that I store in old pill bottles or film containers. Sometimes I label them, and sometimes I don't. I plant a lot of mystery seeds. Some of the seed pods are as lovely as the blossoms — poppy seed pods for one, especially the seed pod of California poppy, at first so small, then becoming long, curved and elegant, and the love-in-a-mist seed heads like small orbs bursting with seed. A clematis that I'd like to get is the *C. tangutica,* a vine that will climb over the fence. It has nodding yellow flowers that become handsome feathery seedheads that last well into winter. I have some seeds pressed between leaded glass, half a dozen flat pale brown seeds with flowing silken tails. It was a present and looks very attractive hanging on the wall.

In the evening at this time of year I rush out and sniff the air like a bloodhound. Frost or no frost? If it's a full moon I'm inclined to go the frost route and rush around the house looking for old sheets and bits of plastic to cover the tomatoes and some of the flowers. Out there in the moonlight with the plants all draped in white, it looks like a garden full of ghosts.

I've also been picking a few Brussels sprouts. Some years ago when the vegetable garden was still littered with massive beams from the old barn we tore down — those beams hung around the garden for years and years — I would leap from beam to beam with a knife between my teeth in search of Brussels sprouts to slice off. I felt quite vicious. Probably because no one would move the damned beams. The tomatoes have never done as well as they did nestled between the large timbers. I think it must have been the warmth and the protection from the wind. In the end I moved the beams myself. A pretty hair-raising job at times. I managed to roll some of them over bit by bit each day, and the smaller ones I sort of tossed, somewhat like tossing the caber! I tossed one onto my toe, though I didn't dare tell anyone. It amazes me what we women are able to put up with — I mean "pain." I'll be telling you about my deliveries soon!

I read somewhere about a man in a grocery store who was buying Brussels sprouts; he turned to another man doing the same and asked him what he should look for in buying them. He said: "Choose the ones that are smiling."

Love, Judy

 Water Lane
West Vancouver, B.C.
September 29

DEAR JUDY,
Palmer strikes again, eh? Hope the hand is better.
These days I think about nothing but tree cutting. It's time

we dealt with some of the overcrowding. We can get rid of several bigleaf maples without any qualms 'cause they were half dead to start with and this dry summer seems to have finished them off. There's a deodar cedar or two we won't miss and a hemlock, a couple of firs and a mountain ash. Although we've decided that Angelica must go, I feel sad whenever I think about it. Her clusters of flowers have turned pink and are studded with pretty rings of tiny black berries, caviar to colourful flocks of robins, flickers, doves and Steller's jays. Good try, Angelica — but do away with a productive walnut? Never!

The biggest trees on the land are the red cedars. They are splendid things — for a forest — but growing a cedar in a suburban garden is like keeping a bald eagle in a chicken coop. Fully grown, they're as tall as fifteen-storey buildings. Their foliage is dense and the roots ruthlessly efficient, so it's hard to grow anything under them. All winter they litter the ground with knobby cone clusters and in fall they shed enough dead fronds to turn a blacktop driveway brown in one night. I know because I've just been out sweeping up.

Our cedars are definitely too big, too greedy and too messy. But when it comes to choosing which trees to remove, there is no doubt in my mind. The cedars must stay.

I wasn't sure, at first, why I felt so strongly, but now I think I understand. It has to do with history. I expect a lot from my garden — certainly more than the odd bunch of carrots. I expect it to be as inspiring as Elgar's cello concerto, and as much fun as the cat. I also depend on it, almost as much as I depend on friends, to give me a sense of belonging. Whenever I've made a major move in my life, it's been my garden that has settled me down, firmed me in, made me feel part of my new surroundings.

Do you ever miss the past? I mean the kind of historic past we grew up with in Britain where life is spent in, on and with the leftovers of countless generations: Roman roads, medieval institutions, Renaissance buildings, Victorian fish forks. Where every inch of soil has been walked over, worked over, fought over, mapped and named. That dense kind of history can be restrictive but it can also be a great comfort and I sometimes wish there were more of it in this part of the world.

I don't remember missing the past so much in New Brunswick. After all, our farmhouse was almost two hundred years old and I was always aware that the land was well worked long before we came on the scene. The little gravestones up on the hill by the vegetable patch were proof of it. I liked having them there — John and Elizabeth McCready and Caleb, who died in 1834 when he was only nineteen. Sometimes while I was picking raspberries or planting cabbages I used to talk to the McCready family (maybe not aloud). I knew they had done the same things in the same place and had felt the way I felt. It was companionable.

There is history here of course but I don't know much about it. It belongs to the First Nations who lived in, on and with the West Coast rain forest. The red cedar symbolised their forest and their culture and they called it the Tree of Life. It clothed them, transported them and housed them. I have the impression the relationship was so intimate, so strong, the story of the people can hardly be separated from the larger story of the forest itself.

But what kind of story does the forest have?

I know (in theory) when this northern rain forest began and I certainly know when large chunks of it came to an end, and that's all; the time between is a blank. It's hard for me to grasp the notion of a history that isn't measured out in decades or reigns — in neat little steps like the rungs of a ladder with us on top. Forest history is one amorphous shape, and legends that tell of its beginnings seem uncannily close to the present.

Our cedars are remnants of the old growth forest which was cleared here only fifty years ago. This is why I have no doubts about keeping them; they are all the history I have. I need them. I think they have something to teach me about this place, if only I can learn.

At night, when the distant grind of traffic has died down, there's a hush in the garden. I sometimes mistake it for silence, but if I take the time to listen, I hear the Trees of Life murmuring. Maybe it's wind in their branches, or the movement of moisture, or the cumulative restlessness of living things. What matters to me is the continuity. These trees are still part of the forest. Their voices began at its beginning and have told its story until now. I don't know the language but sometimes, in the dark, I think I catch a wisp of understanding and when I do, I feel my roots move microscopically deeper.

Love, Elspeth

Kennebecasis River Road
Hampton, N.B.
October 10

DEAR ELSPETH,

Odd that you talked so much about cedars in your last letter.
I was talking on the phone and looking out into the back
garden — a windy day of course — when quite suddenly a
gust took the top off one of the cedars — it's hanging there
like a broken arm. I feel sorry when something happens to
the trees. Heaven knows so many have been cut down
around here. And they take forever to grow.

It's not so much the history I miss, as living in a place
where no one else in my family has lived. I envy groups of
people who talk about their cousins and aunts who've lived
here forever. It's family succession I miss. When I visit
England I don't feel at home there, and I don't feel at home
here. I wonder how long it takes? The boys, even though
they were born in Texas, are true-blue Canadians. I envy
other people's reminiscence that go way back, like:

> *You remember when old Charlie Fry married Mel
> Francis' daughter from up the Narrows, big fat girl
> she was. It was 'er brother that suddenly quit work
> because he said he heard the Lord one night and
> the Lord called him to better things. Charlie Fry
> said, "That weren't the Lord, that were a loon."*

We do have extended family memories. Remember when the
six of us went to Grand Manan for a few days? It rained most
of the time, and we laughed most of the time. We joked

about an elusive figure we called "Roland." Ellen cooked us the best pollack I've ever tasted, and will never forget, and d'you remember on our way to Dark Harbour, we drove up a hill and suddenly on the crest, backlit by sunlight — long blond curls streaming, black-and-red checked shirt billowing, hands firmly on the handlebars of his ATV — was this glory of manhood. We all stopped talking and stared. He seemed poised in this slant of sun — "silent upon a peak." He looked at us, not a tooth in his head, and one of us said, "Roland." How we laughed! It's one of my fondest memories.

Talking of family succession, you know I'm always trying to make out I'm still living in the country and not surrounded by new houses, so I keep planting trees around the edge of the property. Since the maples and lindens have done so well, in summer our thin tall house nearly disappears into the trees. This spring I dug up more small maples from a friend's garden (she knew about this, not a night raid) and planted them in the back area outside the kitchen window. While I was digging the hole, bits of old china caught my eye. On one piece, stamped in green, is the front half of a lion. You can see his two front paws, and beneath it is the name of the manufacturer — JOHN MADDOC — the rest is broken off. It's remarkable that it should appear in our garden when our name is Maddocks and I have a son named Jonathon Maddocks and Tom had an uncle in England called John Maddocks. The china came from England because, also in green, ENG is stamped on it. I dug around but didn't come across matching bits. A chance in a million, but then… I wonder if I should rush out and buy a lotto ticket?

One day I dug up a small round metal coin purse. Inside was a metal disc on a spring which I suppose was meant to

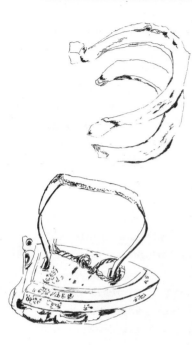

let the coins spring out. I've unearthed many horseshoes along with large nails and rusty hinges. I've also found old toys, small trucks with all the wheels intact, a pretty blue bottle and recently a flatiron with its stand. But it's glass I seem to find more than anything else; in fact glass is my best "crop." I've also lost things in the garden, a ring and a bracelet made of old sixpences. I wonder if someone will find it, say a hundred years from now. And of course I've already told you about the old newspapers I found in the outhouse. I often think of the Honest Rootgatherer.

I was cleaning up my tools and putting them away — not a long job as I don't have all that many — and thought it's a good job that only one of us in this family gardens. If Tom decided to have a go in the garden we'd immediately have all new equipment, a sit-on mower at the very least, the best tools, wheelbarrows galore, garden furniture out of this world and everything done by the book. We would need another shed! But I don't have to worry because he hates to get his hands in the earth, loathes messy or sticky hands. As for me, I love nothing so much as my hands covered with earth.

I wonder how husbands and wives manage if they both garden. Is one always the boss? Is there a division of labour — one flowers, the other vegetables, one cuts the grass, the other the shrubs? How do you manage?

I imagine battles among gardening spouses; with us it would be trench warfare because of the many ditches dug. I see couples running amuck among the pink flamingoes, batterings with spades, counter-attacks with hoses, and curmudgery in the shrubbery, then an armed truce among the love-in-a-mist.

Love, Judy

90

Water Lane
West Vancouver, B.C.
October 19

Dear Judy,
One of the first things I discovered when I started designing gardens was that garden paths can be bumpy for couples and even bumpier for a third party. I've learned to tiptoe until I have a grasp of the personal politics involved and, over the years, I've identified three systems of operation:
   1. Boss and go-fer. One says, "We'll plant it here," and the other goes for the spade, the bone meal, the barrow full of compost, the stake, the string, the secateurs, the beer...
   2. Duty Demarcation. One does the lawn, the other the beds. One does the vegetables, the other the flowers. One does the front garden, the other the back. One puts things into the ground, the other pulls them out.
   3. Do What You Like, Dear, As Long As You Don't:
   Spend money.
   Spend time (which could be better spent cooking / taking out the garbage).
   Whimper when I drive past garden centres.
   Strangely enough, the third system is often preferred by old hands. It offers freedom and a great sense of personal achievement to those with plenty of patience and cunning, those whose backs, knees, elbows, and marriages are sturdy enough to survive. As you know.
   Ray might not agree but I'd say we are the second type. He leans towards potatoes, Swiss chard, pruning fruit trees, digging trenches and (I hope) building stone walls, while I

do the enjoyable parts (i.e., everything else). We don't always see eye to eye on the pruning and we're inclined to need trowels and the wheelbarrow at the same time but otherwise we tread our separate paths peacefully enough. My concept of the ideal gardening partner is one who'll follow in my wake disposing of the weeds I pull out, and I doubt if such a one exists.

October 20

It's amazing, isn't it, what finds its way into garden soil? I never came across anything as interesting as your purse or the flatiron but at the farm we did find some really old coins. The head on one was like a Roman emperor but I couldn't read the date. Once, when I was supervising the construction of a garden area close to a house, the back hoe unearthed a primrose yellow toilet bowl in almost perfect condition. I nearly had a heart attack when the same back hoe dragged up the end of a broken cable. I'm usually particular about checking the position of underground cables before letting back hoes loose on a property, but in this case I'd been too busy checking the position of overhead branches, wires and eaves. Luckily for me, the cable in question was nothing but a scrap, unattached to anything. It taught me a lesson though.

We've counted more than twenty trees that are diseased, dead or hopelessly overcrowded. The trunk of one sickly fir is far too big to reach my arms around and I can't imagine how such a big tree can be felled without crushing a great swath of garden, ours or Anne's. What we need is a lumberjack with good insurance coverage. We picked three names from the phone book, asked for estimates and have chosen the young man who came most promptly.

A week or so ago we saw a squirrel scampering boldly along the railings of the deck. Then we saw another squirrel. And another. We were amused at first and so was Moses — at first — but a chubby cat is no match for nutbound squirrels and, for the last two weeks, Moses has lain about the deck assuming postures of frank apathy while overhead, a steady stream of walnuts has flitted off into the bush. In desperation, we tied a few choice clusters in little bags of flyscreen netting but squirrel wits and teeth are sharp, and it looks as if we'll end up without a single nut. Hmmm!

October 24

The tree cutters have been and gone, leaving the garden resoundingly quiet, strangely airy and only a little tattered. They worked non-stop all afternoon then rushed off to tackle another job. I rushed off to sink into an armchair.

I had misgivings at first about our man's youth and his less-than-lumberjack build, but I needn't have worried. I was wide-eyed with admiration as he skipped up the side of the fir with the help of spiked footwear and a belt slung around the trunk. He carried a chain-saw and trimmed off the branches as he went. I watched from a discreet distance until all I could see against the dazzle of sky was a small black shape at the top of a tapering pole. He worked his way back down from his dizzy perch, slicing the trunk off in neat firewood sized chunks which dropped harmlessly to the ground while his crew whisked the branches away to be fed into a chipper.

In next to no time the maples, hemlocks, cedars and rowan had disappeared. I took one last look at Walnut and Angelica.

I couldn't put it off any longer.

"Which one?" asked the nimble young executioner with the chain-saw. I pointed and turned away. Fifteen minutes later, when the hideous sound had faded, I looked back.

Slash and a neat pile of logs were all that remained of a sturdy young walnut. Do you think Sophie will ever forgive me?

Angelica has been blatantly triumphant. She blushed pink and gold all over. She glowed. She strutted her stuff in fine style, then overnight, and with her usual flare for farce, she threw off all her finery and stood brazenly naked, knee-deep in leafy debris.

So that's why I'm sitting here looking across the deck at something resembling a hat rack.

Love, Elspeth

 Kennebecasis River Road
Hampton, N.B.
November 9

DEAR ELSPETH
So you've killed the walnut. I don't think I'll tell Sophie, she won't be happy with you. You'll have to send her some walnuts for Christmas. And thinking of Christmas — the snow has just started. And I love it. The first fall is always exciting; something different. It skims across the front lawn and eddies around the trees and shrubs, large lush flakes. Soon hard edges will be rounded, debris hidden from sight and noise muffled by the soft shroud of winter. (Did I read that somewhere?)

And the garden will sleep soundly under snow. If this were only so, instead of the thawing and freezing we get here. It's

not the snow I mind, it's the ice. It's so hard on plants. I
daren't think of the perennials I've planted and never seen
again, like my brother who took in two stray cats and had
them spayed. He brought them home from the vet, opened
the car door, the cats shot out and disappeared forever. I
coddle new perennials with milk crates, old buckets and
bales of hay, and at the first sign of spring, peer down at
them calling their names, but only their labels remain.
Sounds like markers in a graveyard, doesn't it? Well,
gardening is often sad and disappointing… not unlike life.
Sometimes the perennials surprise me and pop up
somewhere else, but not as often as I'd like.

   At the first fall of snow, cars drive cautiously; if this were
April they'd be whipping along in spite of the slippery roads.
If we had selective snowing — none on the roads and
driveways and all concentrated on the gardens, fields and
hills — I'd like it even more.

   I can see the daisies that I staked in one of the front beds;
I tied them with elastic, wide elastic. I don't know why I
chose elastic; it probably chose me by being
close at hand. In the wind the daisies look
like sled dogs pulling hard at the traces.
The large rose bush outside the garage
door is heavy with wet snow and the
shiny hips looks like brilliant red
Christmas lights.
Both bushes of
honeysuckle on the
south side of the
house have slipped
their tethers.

One was tied to the garage wall and the other was fastened to stakes pushed into the ground. Before the first bush broke free it looked like a horse shaking its massive head from side to side in an effort to get rid of its halter. Both bushes now have broken free. I wonder where they think they're off to? The main stems seem quite strong and I hope flexible, but I don't like the way they're bending lower and lower. Snow is outlining the stems and branches, and the temperature is just below freezing, so I don't think it will last.

The string I used for the honeysuckles was a lovely green garden twine I got in Maine, a large ball that made me feel as though I knew what I was about. It was so nice to handle, but obviously I was seduced by its colour and texture because it's not holding well at all. Maybe I didn't tie it securely enough. Before putting the string around the stems I wrapped them with plastic bags to prevent the string from cutting into them, but I see that the plastic bags are doing a fair bit of flapping. Perhaps the honeysuckles are planning to run off with all their goods and chattels in the plastic bags! That's what the first fall of snow does for you, loosens your mind!

Later:

When the snow and the wind stopped I went out into the transformed garden, now white and silent, the snow the texture of soap flakes. I looked at the honeysuckles; parts of the string were broken and knots had slipped off the nails. Both bushes seemed heavy and cumbersome; if the weather is good tomorrow I'll try and tie them again.

Between the stones in the walls: hen-and-chicks tucked in white blankets, clumps of hosta yellow against the snow, and

the dark stems and scant purple petals of coneflowers, still handsome.

At the base of each tree was a collar of snow and around the foot of each trunk a hollowed-out space; I've often wondered — is this because of the wind or the warmth from the tree? Cones of snow sat on upturned water barrels; snow outlined the rounded surfaces of the wood pile, turning it into a judge's wig. The weight of snow on the branches of pines changed them into ballerinas; the bird feeder was topped by candyfloss and seed heads of bee balm wore pointed white caps.

A late-flowering clematis near the back door was frozen. Its dark red petals held small offerings of snow, as though inviting me to share in the feast.

Out on the marsh, snow had collected on the thin ice circling the shrubby islands; they looked as though dressed in frilly white skirts.

You will miss all this, this immediate covering up and hiding away of the garden, the sudden disappearance of all the rubbish you never managed to clean up. Snow has its advantages, but then there are the months and months of waiting for spring. I've heard it whispered, snow does sometimes fall on Vancouver, then all life is disrupted.

The plow has just rumbled by on its first run this winter.

Love, Snowmaiden

Water Lane
West Vancouver, B.C.
November 23

DEAR JUDY,
I've always loved the view from your place; you have the
ideal combination of trees and water. And I know just what
you mean by the frilly white skirts round the islands. Wasn't
it Christo, the installation artist, who put pink skirts around
islands in Biscayne Bay off the Florida coast? I've seen
photos of them and they weren't a patch on your marshes.

When we began house hunting, the first thing we learned
was that VIEW in Vancouver means a sight of the ocean. Next
thing we learned was that we couldn't afford one. Vancouver
views seem to be more a question of quantity than quality,
and I have the impression that property values in some areas
are calculated by the linear foot of visible horizon.

My first garden was in the Shetland Islands, where views
of the sea are commonplace but trees are rare. Perhaps that's
why I love to look out at trees in all their moods. Here, trees
aren't a view; they're more of a threat. The worst crime a tree
can commit is to come between the viewer and that
extremely expensive strip of sea. I'm exaggerating of course,
but only a little. Not everyone in Vancouver is afflicted with
ocean view madness and tree phobia, but there are those
who sneak onto public land at night armed with chain-saws,
and I've even heard of people eliminating trees while the
owners are on holiday.

When I looked in the Yellow Pages for tree cutters I was
astonished by the number of companies advertising tree
removal and topping. It was my introduction to a strange

local custom.

Most societies harbour at least one inexplicable tradition; maybe we all need a little craziness in our lives. When we lived in Shetland, we took part every year in a jamboree that involved building a boat, dragging it through the streets and setting it alight. In New Brunswick they set fire to the grass. In Vancouver they shimmy up trees and chop the tops off.

Why? I've been told here that tall trees are more likely to fall over than topped ones. But that doesn't make sense to me. When the main trunk of a tree is cut off, the branches below the cut grow with extra vigour, so unless you keep hacking, you're soon back where you started, only worse. You've made a sort of Hydra, a multi-headed monster. What's more, the neck wound is forever open to fungal attack and a sick tree really can be dangerous. Side wounds made by the removal of branches are sealed off by the tree's own defences so, if a tree must be reduced because of wind, side branches should be removed in a spiral. But try telling that to a topper!

On Vancouver's North Shore the land rises steeply from the sea and houses sit in tiers above each other. A tall tree causes more consternation than a large hat at the theatre. The municipal authorities have produced a booklet to promote short-growing trees, but I still see people planting types that will be giants in a few years.

Now I've come across another custom. Windowing. This means cutting branches to allow views *through* a tree. As you can imagine, after topping and windowing, there isn't much tree left.

The bank at the side of the driveway is finally regraded. I've added topsoil and have just been out planting young shrub roses. Do I miss the snow? Right now its advantages escape me completely. But we haven't entirely escaped a sense of impending winter. Both Ray and I have felt an urgent need to prepare for the worst. I've been resisting the temptation to stock up with food and to knit mittens. Ray has been fussing with firewood as if we still depended on a wood stove. He has unearthed the snow shovels and the scoops, which he brought from New Brunswick, and given half a chance I think he'd rush around stacking hay bales against the foundations of the house. At the farm, our survival depended on such preparations and I doubt if we'll ever get over this nervous fall feeling, even if winter proves to be nothing more than a few chilly weeks in January.

Love, Elspeth

 Kennebecasis River Road
Hampton, N.B.
December 3

DEAR ELSPETH,
It must be catching; I have to get some trees cut down. But I don't have to choose between exotic names like *Juglans regia* or *Japanese angelica,* nor do I have to worry about culling, just cutting. I know if I asked a "tree-cutter" in New Brunswick to top or window a tree, he'd look at me and say, "I've never heard tell o' that," and that would be the end of it.

Back at the beginning of November I was worried; the wind was just roaring past the house and a large limb from a very dead elm had blown off. Bits of bark were flying all over the place. I phoned N.B. Power to see if they would take the elms down as they seemed close to the power lines. They'd come and inspect, they said.

These trees are the last of about ten elms that have all succumbed to Dutch elm disease. Several years ago, when the first ones were cut down, I was so upset I had to leave the house for the day. When I got home, I saw that a large tree was lying across the snow, cut up into bite-size pieces. It looked like the vertebrae of a dinosaur. I found a branch with a Baltimore oriole's nest hanging from it — you know the one I mean, a lovely silvery pouch.

Anyway, to get back to my immediate problem. Last week a man from the power company came about the trees. He gave me his card. Vegetation Supervisor, it said. I imagined him going through rows of cabbage and broccoli with a whip, telling them to shape up. I pointed out the dead trees, one newly dead very close to a power line and the two others, dead a long time, not as close.

"We'll take that one," he said of the newly dead. We tramped through the lilac bushes to the others. He looked me up and down and said: "We'll take a limb."

I thought he meant mine.

"What about the rest of the tree?" I asked.

"You want the rest cut down?"

"Well, yes," I said.

"Have to take it up with the contractor."

"How much will it cost?" I asked. He told me. An arm and a leg! He said he had to go to Grand Manan but if I needed him there was his phone number. I've never needed a Vegetation Supervisor before, but who knows, I just might.

A few days later he appeared on my front lawn again, this time with another man. I went out to see what was going on. His crony said: "I remember you. You wouldn't let us take that big maple."

This was June, a year ago. They had wanted to cut down a healthy maple in order to install a hydro pole. There had been a bit of a fuss. Why take a beautiful maple when we were surrounded by dead and dying elms? In the end I kept the maple and the pole was erected further away.

Both men were wearing blue hard hats and dayglo vests. The men inspected the trees and measured the trunks with their arms. I traipsed behind them into the lilac bushes. The crony still seemed interested in the maple and I didn't want any mistakes, like, "Whoopsie, there goes that maple." They angled up the trees and peered around them; I thought they were playing hide-and-seek.

"We'll put a rope to 'er," they said. Then they sprayed a big red C on the trunks.

"That's for Cut," said the Vegetation Supervisor. I thought it was for Christmas.

He told me they'd be back when the ground was frozen, with not too much snow and no wind. An unlikely combination. He asked if he'd given me his card.

Love, Judy

P.S. I hope you like this year's Christmas card. The Crowley's Camperdown elm dusted with snow.

Water Lane
West Vancouver, B.C.
December 11

DEAR JUDY,
A Vegetation Supervisor is exactly what I need to help tame this garden. You could send him as my Christmas present.

Believe it or not, it's snowing here and, as you predicted, all life is disrupted. People who live higher up the North Shore mountains have been calling the radio station in a panic to warn that door steps are slippery. They have *two centimetres* of the treacherous white stuff on the ground and it's *still falling*. Almost a state of emergency. Down here at sea level, most of the flakes are melting as they touch down but when I looked out of the bedroom window first thing this morning there were patches of white among the new shrub roses. At first I couldn't think what they were but once I realised it wasn't litter (the raccoons getting into the garbage again) I decided it looked rather pretty, with the masses of tiny red hips on the roses, the dark green of the bearberry and the bright green of the *Centranthus*.

I wonder if *Centranthus* would survive with you. I'll send you seed to try. I planted a few clumps on the roadside and along the driveway. I love it, though it seeds itself with abandon. The seeds are like small dandelion parachutes and I'm not sure how far they are likely to travel. To be on the safe side I must remember, next summer, to cut off the flower heads before too many of them take to the air. The leaves are fresh green and soft looking; not leaves you'd expect to be evergreen but here we are, almost the darkest day of the year, and they look fine. At least from an upstairs window.

I hope the holly and ivy have arrived in good condition. According to my book about the language of flowers, holly means *Am I forgotten?* and a sprig of ivy with tendrils means *Eager to please.* Both appropriate! There are several hollies in the garden but only the big one at the back of the pond has berries. You may notice that some of the ivy has berries too and different leaves. Curious that both plants have peculiar sex lives.

Did you know that the ordinary ivy with triple pointed leaves and a climbing habit is only the juvenile form? When an ivy gets down to the business of reproduction, the leaves change into plainer, bulkier shapes and it loses all ambition to climb. Come to think of it, something like this happened to me too. Cuttings taken from the mature part of the plant keep the bushy habit and are used for hedges, though I've heard it's hard to root them. It's one of those things I mean to try but probably never will. Most flowering plants have both male and female parts built in but hollies, like yew and date palm, have either one or the other. My holly is female and if I want her to keep producing berries I'll have to leave a male tree nearby. To complicate matters more, everything I've just written about flowering plants is, strictly speaking, untrue!

Did you realise that the plants we grow in our gardens are, in reality, sexless? It's the next generation (a hidden generation of spores) that's sexy. Our berry-bearing holly doesn't really have a gender; it's only a producer of tiny female ovules which have sex with tiny male pollen grains from the non-berry-bearing trees. This means our plants are more like grandparents, than parents to their seeds. Chaste grandparents. At this point I feel confused. Aren't animals the same? Does this make me a grandparent already? Perhaps the best thing to do is put the holly and the ivy on the mantlepiece, hang mistletoe above the door and be grateful that intellectual understanding, while nice, is not essential to most of life's pleasures.

We have good reasons to celebrate this festive season. Jean and Charles are coming from England for Christmas and are planning to move to Vancouver next year. We're absolutely delighted. I think Jean will stay on after Christmas and look for a place to live while Charles winds up his business in London. Also, I'm quitting my job in the city. Ray and I are going to start our own practice again. We'll turn the big ground floor room into an office and we're hoping to enlarge it in the spring. Ray has designed a much needed face-lift for the house, and I'm making sure that a greenhouse is included somewhere in the plans, though it may be years before it becomes a reality.

Sadly, Kate and Paul can't afford to fly over for Christmas and I've just been making up a parcel of goodies for them. We'll miss them and we'll also miss the traditions of a

Christmas season with old friends. I've been thinking about the song and dance act we did at the New Year's Eve play at Hooper's. If I didn't have the photographs to prove it, I wouldn't believe we sang those ridiculous songs dressed as penguins and didn't even trip over our frogman flippers.

Will the family be home? Has Jonathan started a new job yet? Does David like living in Toronto? You'll be so pleased to have them back.

Merry Christmas, all of you!
And Happy New Year from all of us here.

 Kennebecasis River Road
Hampton, N.B.
January 4

Dear Elspeth,
Thank goodness Christmas has come and gone. I've always had a fear that some disaster will befall a member of our family at Christmas and am always relieved when it's all over. And of course there's all the extra cooking, which as you know is something I can do without. I was in the launderette just before Christmas — our washer had frozen again — and in came Hildegard's husband. I can never remember his name — it's something like Caligula or Caliban. He said that Hildegard had gone to visit her mother who was sick. The radio was on and an administrator was being interviewed. The man had numbers and projected numbers right at his finger tips.

"That really impresses me," Caliban said, tapping his forehead. "A man who can come out with numbers just like that. All up here."

"Caliban," I said, "that doesn't impress me at all. It's women who come up with meals for three hundred and sixty-five days a year that impress me."

"Oh no no no," he said, "that's nothing, nothing." And he held up his underwear with a pattern of Santa Claus riding on a sleigh stamped on it. He threw them in the washer and yelled, "Ho, Ho, Ho."

This year, only David came home. Didn't I tell you? In October, Jonathan dumped his job in Toronto and with five others took an eighteen-metre catamaran from Oregon down to Mexico — plenty of room for disaster right there. He expects to be on the high seas for six months. We've had two phone calls, one from California because something broke and another from Mexico, where he was wearing shorts. Couldn't wear shorts here, bitterly cold. David said he was freezing all the time, in spite of a roaring woodstove, furnace up high and a hot water bottle in his bed. In the night, he moved his bed to the middle of the room because he said he wanted to get out of the wind! Didn't know that Toronto was that much warmer? His apartment must be.

Two of our neighbours came for Christmas dinner. Now they really impress me. One is ninety and the other close, and both are very sharp. The older one decided this year to get rid of her car. It was a 1976 in great shape — like them. It had never been driven in winter because she spent winters in Florida; she stays home now, because she doesn't want to die there. In summer they have a nice garden; their pansies always come back. Where mine go I have no idea.

We didn't expect a white Christmas but we got one. And the snow hasn't stopped. I was out there clearing off the path and scooped up a clump of creeping thyme by mistake and put it in water in the house. I have some potting soil and will pot it up, just to see if I can save it. It reminded me of the first winter I spent in Canada after coming up from the southern States. One bitter February day I thought I'd repot a jade plant. I put it on top of the car and was going to search for earth. It turned out I didn't need earth at all; the cold had turned the jade into what looked like a bunch of wizened grapes. Oh, and before I forget, thanks so much for the holly. It arrived in perfect condition. I have some friends in North Carolina who also send me greenery at Christmas; their gaylax and your holly came on the same day. Gaylax has dark green shiny heart-shaped leaves, and stays green year-round in North Carolina. It always reminds me of the friends with whom I hiked every week when I lived there. We'd hike for fifteen or twenty kilometres, sometimes on the Appalachian Trail or in the Smokies. I think those hikes, the laughing and talking, came close to being some of the best times of my life.

You mentioned *Centranthus* looking so green in your little dabs of snow. I wonder how it would do here? It's valerian, isn't it? I see it's for zones 5 to 7. Sown as an annual it might be OK. I think I've tried it but it's never popped up the next year.

I've just had some mulled wine and am enjoying a lovely little gardening book David gave me for Christmas. It's full of gardening folklore and is such a pleasure to handle. It's called *A Miscellany of Garden Wisdom* and was compiled by

Bernard Schofield. And the verse on the front is by Reginald Arkell:

> *I think it must be rather nice*
> *To live by giving good advice;*
> *To talk of what the garden needs,*
> *Instead of pulling up the weeds.*

It tells of the merits of dung; it says that you can turn pink or white hydrangeas blue by burying rusty nails in the soil; that the planting of leather, such as found in old shoes, is an effective manure for peach trees; and yes, read this: "The Egyptian and Greek instructions of Husbandry... the seeds shall be committed to the earth when the Moon possesseth her half light or is a quarter old." What a lovely phrase: *When the Moon possesseth her half light*. In a preamble it says you should sow with a waxing moon. Well, old Caliban was out there at the wrong time then. I wonder if he knew this little gem: "indulging in sexual intercourse among crops... was performed to increase the fertility of plants." I can see him romping with Hildegard among the scarlet runners.

I've had a very pleasant evening reading this book and drinking the last of the mulled wine, but must finish because *the moon possesseth her half light*.

> *Happy new year,*
> *Love, Judy*

Water Lane
West Vancouver, B.C.
January 12

DEAR JUDY,
What an adventure Jonathan is having! Mexico keeps
cropping up these days. Kimi's brother works there and he
flew up here for a few days around New Year. It was great to
meet him and he managed to communicate very well in a
sort of Japanese Spanglish.

We loved having Jean and Charles here too and, of course,
Rob and Kimi came out from town for Christmas Day. It's
maybe a good thing Kate wasn't here because she's a devoted
traditionalist and wouldn't have approved of my Christmas
dinner. We had Christmas soup. Honestly! Leek and potato.
But with chopped parsley and swirls of cream it didn't look
too shabby and for the first time in thirty years I savoured
Christmas day without forebodings of underdone turkey and
overdone Brussels sprouts.

We broke with another tradition too. No tree. And no
excuse except that I didn't feel like it. I went to the
December meeting of a local garden club and the
programme featured a flower arranger making Christmas
displays in an ingenious variety of containers. One was a
short section of eaves trough. As soon as I saw it I knew I'd
found the perfect Christmas tree substitute. There was
consternation among the younger generation when I
proposed a Christmas Eaves Trough. Where would the
presents go? But Ray suddenly caught the spirit of the thing
and produced a length of aluminum troughing, cut to fit the
full length of the mantlepiece, with ends clipped on and

neatly sealed. I bought three blocks of florist's foam, cut them in half and spaced them along its length. If I'd bought six and left them whole I'd have had an easier time hiding the trough. But the Scot will out.

Searching the garden for trimmings of greenery was much more enjoyable than poking round the attic for boxes of Christmas lights. I don't mean to gloat, but I still get a thrill from the variety of evergreens I can grow here. Think of it: Mexican orange blossom, *Escallonia, Daphne, Pieris*, to say nothing of holly and ivy.

If your temperature is below -20°C you probably shouldn't read this next bit.

The best of all was the *Viburnum tinus*. I have two types: a compact one, 'Spring Bouquet', and a robust form. Both have berries like blue metallic beads, and pinkish white flowers. Yes, flowers. They were in full bloom and deliciously fragrant when I brought them into the house. I have another *Viburnum* in flower too. It's a hybrid developed at Bodnant in Wales and it's called *bodnantense* 'Dawn'. Its flowers are brighter pink and even more fragrant but the shrub is deciduous so I didn't use it in the trough. I'm traditional enough to feel that festive boughs should be green.

When all the bits and pieces were arranged in the wet foam I put in two dark red candles and felt pretty smug. Then Ray brought home some gorgeous pink lilies and I added them and decided the world doesn't get much better. I think Ray felt a proprietary interest in the whole thing by this time because, when the lilies wilted after a week in the heat of the yule logs, he replaced them with a large stem of orchids.

I've never had an orchid before and felt this one should be

commemorated so I've been painting its portrait, a little at a time when the spirit moves me. Luckily orchids are wonderfully long lasting. Strangely, as this one ages, its flowers are withering at random — not like delphiniums from bottom to top, or like the spikes of *Liatris* from top to bottom.

I read something interesting recently about flower spikes, the bottom to top kind. The lower flowers have little or no pollen but plenty of nectar, so bees start low and work up. The upper flowers have little or no nectar but plenty of pollen, so when the bees fly off to find more rewarding bottom flowers, they are well dusted with pollen. This little trick makes it less likely that a plant will self-pollinate and more likely that cross-pollination will occur — a healthier situation in evolutionary terms.

But to get back to our non-traditional Christmas…

Just in case you think I've been attending self-assertion classes or something equally Lotus Land, I should admit I cooked a turkey with trimmings for twelve on Boxing Day.

I hope the scooped-up thyme survives. If not I'll send some in the spring.

I'm so happy to be working at home again. It'll be tough starting from scratch but we have enough work to keep us going for a few weeks and we're used to the insecurity of private practice.

Keep warm!

Love, Elspeth

Kennebecasis River Road
Hampton, N.B.
January 25

DEAR ELSPETH,
Christmas Eaves Trough! And you know what day it is today,
don't you? Burns Day. Instead of haggis I suppose it will be
macaroni sandwiches? And for Valentine's Day will it be
kidneys instead of hearts? All day I've been trying to sing,
"My love is like a red red rose," and said to Tom, "I wish I
could sing in tune," and he said, "So do I."

   I have thought about artificial trees, but you know the
economy of New Brunswick depends on tree cutting and I'd
hate to upset that! I overheard two women discussing real
versus artificial trees. One of them said she nearly bought an
artificial one, but her daughter, who had come from
Australia for Christmas, said: "I didn't come all this way for
an artificial tree."

   We had quite a fright the other night. The house was on
fire. About two in the morning Tom discovered the attic was
full of smoke so called the fire department. God love 'um,
they were here in minutes swarming all over the house and
even out on the roof, which as you know, is very steep. The
temperature was -21°C but luckily there was no wind. The
firemen ran their hands up and down the chimney looking
for hot spots — sounds like a nightclub — and found one
behind the woodstove in the kitchen. They stood around
with hoses at the ready and discussed how they should hack
the tiles off the wall. D'you remember the fire in *A Child's
Christmas in Wales* when the aunt comes into the room, sees
the firemen and says: "Would you like anything to read?" I

was sorely tempted. Anyway, behind the tiles was a large timber about to burst into flames. They hauled it out and threw it into the ice cold night. It glowed for hours in the snow. We were really lucky the entire place didn't go up in smoke.

The cold snap has now given way to the January thaw; no snow and temperatures around 10°C with rain and wind. I was out there just now and the metal labels I've sprinkled around the garden are bent double as if they have stomach ache. I saw some of my hay mulch running off down the road and even the wood chips are whirling around.

Thanks for the Louise Beebe Wilder book. She mentions a garden in Llandaff, Wales, which is not far from where I was born. It was a white flower garden, and she lists all the plants that grow in succession. Since the book was published in 1935 I wonder if the garden still exists. There is a dahlia called 'Bishop of Llandaff' that I've been tempted to buy. It's a red single flower that looks lovely in the photographs but it grows about a metre high, and wouldn't stand a chance here in the wind. I was confirmed by the Bishop of Llandaff, but alas it didn't take.

I used to dislike white flowers because they reminded me of winter. I changed my mind when I realized how well they stand out in the dusk. I once read that white blossoms attract moths which in turn fertilize the plants in the evening. Also, white flowers look cool in a hot summer. I'm hoping some day to have a white peony; last year I bought one that's supposed to be white; I hope it is, but if it flowers at all I'll be happy, never mind the colour. Interesting the bit about flower spikes and the upper blossoms having nectar. *Lavatera* 'Mont Blanc' is one of my favourite annuals. Each

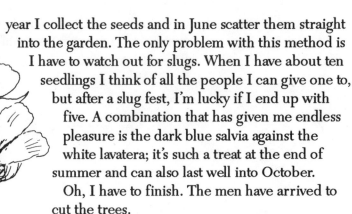

year I collect the seeds and in June scatter them straight into the garden. The only problem with this method is I have to watch out for slugs. When I have about ten seedlings I think of all the people I can give one to, but after a slug fest, I'm lucky if I end up with five. A combination that has given me endless pleasure is the dark blue salvia against the white lavatera; it's such a treat at the end of summer and can also last well into October.

Oh, I have to finish. The men have arrived to cut the trees.

Love, Judy

 Kennebecasis River Road
Hampton, N.B.
January 26, and so it continues

Yes, they're out there now — three of them, all in different coloured hats, but no Vegetation Supervisor.

A young guy clad all in orange, like an Orange Julius, seems to be in charge of the chain-saw. I talked to a blue-hatted man while Orange Julius cased the elms in among the lilacs. Blue Hat said, "We'll put a rope around her," nodding in the direction of the lilac bushes. As soon as he spoke we heard a chain-saw, then a loud crack, and Blue Hat ran for a hooked pole and the man in the Yellow Hat raced for a rope. But too late, the tree slowly fell. "I guess we won't use a rope," said Blue Hat. "So rotten you could've pushed her over with yer shoulder."

They used ropes for the next one; one rope was attached to the front of the truck, another through a pulley up in the tree, and other pieces of rope around some spruce trees. They backed the truck down the road, tightening up the rope, then Orange Julius started the chain-saw. The ropes jumped and, slowly at first, with a splintering sound, the tree toppled down. After that, they sat in their truck which was parked in our driveway. I thought they were discussing strategy, but no, they were discussing lunch.

After lunch it was Blue Hat's turn with the chain-saw. I can see him from the window. He's going up to the top of the remaining elm in a cherry picker and seems to be doing tricks with a rope; he attaches it to a limb — not his limb — and throws a length of it to the ground. Oh, Yellow Hat, the oldest of the trio, has just slipped on the ice in the ditch. Orange Julius says something to him and laughs, then Yellow Hat flicks him across the behind with the end of the rope. And they both laugh. They slot the end of the rope through a hook beneath the other truck and Yellow Hat drives it down next door's driveway until it is taut. Blue Hat is sawing a V-shaped notch in the tree. Next he saws away at the other side; Orange Julius holds onto the rope as a huge limb thuds to the ground. They seem to have a lot of control over the felling, except maybe for the first one that came down in a bit of a hurry, and nobody yells, "timber... r... r." They gradually de-limb the tree so that only the large trunk remains. They saw the trunk across the bottom, and it too is guided down with the rope, neatly into the ditch.

Now that all the tall elms have gone the sky looks so empty. They used to remind me of fan vaulting in a cathedral. A number of years ago when the elms started to die I planted maples so the area isn't completely bare. There is also an ash among them, and two ornamental cherries. The maples have done well and give privacy in summer, and as I mentioned to you before, I've made flower beds around some of the trees and also around one of the stumps in my effort to disguise it.

Later:
The Vegetation Supervisor has just come by to see if everything went off OK. I told him I thought the men were very efficient and asked him how I could get rid of the massive stumps. He said, "Find a fellah with a big back hoe."

Love, Judy

 Water Lane
West Vancouver, B.C.
February 2

DEAR JUDY,
Fire! I'm so glad you're both alright, and the house too. But I can imagine what a mess it has made of your kitchen and your *beautiful tiles* — after all the time and hard work it took getting them up there!
Fancy losing your tiles and your elms all in one month. I liked your blow by blow account of the elms' demise but I'm sad they've gone. I'll always think of your place as the tall house surrounded with elms.
The ice on the pond has thawed and some of the goldfish have reappeared. They aren't very lively but at least they're

floating the right way up. I don't know what has happened to the rest of the shoal. The raccoons, kingfishers and herons are an ever present danger and all the ideas I've come up with for outwitting them are either unsightly (fish netting suspended from poles) or ineffective (trip wires round the edge) or, as in the case of our pink flamingo painted grey, both.

When Charles was here, he told us he was staring out of the kitchen window thinking, in a vague sort of way, that our painted flamingo made a pretty good-looking heron, when suddenly it rose up and flapped off.

I'm not sure when fish feed again after their winter rest but I don't want to risk starting yet because they stand out so brilliantly orange against the black water. Soon the water surface will be smothered with lily leaves and then it's easier for them to hide, so I think I'll wait a few weeks before I give them their daily pinch of Swimmy Baby.

When Kimi's mother came over for the wedding, she brought us wonderful presents including several years' supply of Japanese fish food. The product must be intended for the Western market because the packaging is in English — well almost:

> *Swimmy Baby will bring your goldfish brighter
>   and attractive.*
> *Swimmy Baby has floating characteristic.*
> *Swimmy Baby imparts highest digestibility.*

And wonder of wonders, it has and it does.

I've been puzzled by the absence of frogs and toads here. I don't know if this has something to do with the world-wide decline in amphibian populations, or if they simply haven't discovered our pond. Apart from the fish, you'd think it would be an ideal spot for them.

After we dug the pond at the farm, we could hardly sleep in the spring for the racket of croaks and grunts, and the chorus of peepers was like a whistling kettle always on the boil. I miss them.

Did you know that we used to have a toad living in the greenhouse there? I can't remember if it wandered in by itself or if I put it there. I encouraged it to stay by providing a saucer of water for wallowing. One spring, when I was digging the tomato bed, I turned over a large clod of earth and was about to whack it with the spade when it rolled over and blinked. I could hardly bring myself to look more closely in case I'd amputated something. What a relief when he crawled off in one piece!

The greenhouse door was often left open, so Toad was free to come and go, and when we didn't see him for about a year we assumed he'd gone. Then one morning I discovered a single, neat, torpedo-shaped dropping on the step. It looked far too big for a toad but according to our nifty book on animal tracking, that's exactly what it was.

I wonder what has become of him now; I hear the Wards have taken down the greenhouse to enlarge the patio. Pity I didn't bring Toad with us — the black beetles and I could certainly do with some help in the slug wars.

I've become extremely slug conscious (Jean says slug obsessed) since I arrived here. I'm always on the lookout for new defences and I read the other day that copper gives them an electric shock, so I'm going to make copper rings out of strapping for some of my more precious plants. You might like to try a copper fence around your *Lavatera* seedlings. I'm not convinced it'll work, but like copper bracelets for arthritis, at least it can't do any harm.

My New Year's resolution is to tackle the whole pond area. I love ponds and I'm looking forward to working on this one. It's a pleasantly irregular shape and not much more than knee-deep in the middle. The fabric liner seems to be in good condition but it's bordered with small rocks which are sliding into the water. My first job will be to rebuild the edge with the largest most natural-looking stones I can lay my hands on. Rob has always enjoyed mucking about with water so I'm hoping he'll give me a hand with that part.

Our whole property slopes down from front to back and, at the back end of the pond, the ground falls away quickly. Too quickly. It feels wrong. The land should look as if it's holding the water securely cupped, so I've decided to raise the ground around the bottom end. I've already started using up the gravelly fill left over from the rose bank regrading (I once told a client that she needed fill to raise part of her garden and she said, "Phil who?"). I know we should build a retaining wall first, then backfill later, but we simply don't have time for walls right now. Funny, isn't it, with garden construction, how something always needs to be done before you can do what you're really trying to do!

I like the idea that a pond is the eye of a garden. At the moment, this eye is closed. So many trees and shrubs overhang it, and so much stuff grows in it, there are no reflections to tell its mood. I want to open it up, give it a

121

glimpse of blue sky, let it sparkle. I want to see it dreamy in the dusk, or pale and mysterious in moonlight. So far, the fish have been my excuse for letting the lilies and pond weed take over but the truth is, I can't face the thought of wading in and tackling the roots. I'm not even sure how I'll do it without damaging the liner and stirring up enough mud to suffocate every living creature in there. The thought of draining the whole thing is equally daunting.

It'll be easier to deal with the vegetation on land. Apart from the walnut and a rowan, which we took down last year, there were five trees in the area. One was an old cherry, diseased and too coarse for this part of the garden which I see as a sort of parlour, intimate and full of pretty colours and dainty nick-nacks. Another was a young *Aralia*, a daughter of Angelica. She had to go. One prima donna is enough. Digging out her roots was a bigger job than we bargained for. Another case for that fellah with a big back hoe.

The pond looks better already with some breathing space round it but when the trees went, some of the mystery went with them. The whole layout became visible at one glance. By putting back a few large plants at strategic points I'm hoping to hide parts of the path again and recapture some of the old feeling of exploration as I walk around it.

You can probably tell I'm enjoying myself...

Love, Elspeth

Kennebecasis River Road
Hampton, N.B.
February 15

DEAR ELSPETH,
We too have been having a thaw. Water everywhere. Last
night the wind sprang up and the temperature rose. In bed I
listened to the different sounds. At first the harsh sound of
ice pellets being flung on the roof, then the wind roaring
like a plane taking off. Later into the morning, when things
had calmed a bit, the wind against the house sounded like
the soft tread of a ballerina.

The ditches along the road are all running brown. Outside
the back door, the new grass I'd planted in the fall was
swaying like seaweed in the water that had accumulated
there; it looked such a vivid green with everything else
brown. I was watching a vole, who lives in a hole in the wall,
darting out to seek higher ground. I saw him scampering
from one island to another. It reminded me of some purple
prose I once read: "Feather-footed through the splashy fen,
goes the questing vole." Can't you just see him in a little
paper boat with a flag, rowing furiously to escape? He was
eyeing the basement. If he thinks it's any drier down there
he's mistaken, because I hear water pouring in. Fortunately
there are runnels on either side of the basement floor and
the water eventually flows out.

While waiting for the rain to stop I thought I'd make
marmalade. Well, I've now been making it for hours. Still
runny! But a lovely smell. One time I made marmalade that
was so hard you couldn't get it out of the jar, but the taste,
after you'd wrestled it into your mouth, was delicious. The

best I've ever made. My day wouldn't be complete without its series of failures.

The rain stopped for a few minutes so I went out into the garden. In the fall I built up piles of leaves; I laboured long at this job, raking and carting them in the wheelbarrow and then putting sacking and metal grids over them so the wind wouldn't blow it all away. At times the wind gusted so hard, I had to throw myself across the pile to save it. I was trying to make leaf mould. Not a complicated procedure like making marmalade. But today the sacking was nowhere to be seen and neither were the leaves. So much for my leaf mould.

If I ever move from this house, from the garden really, I'd look for a place out of the wind. Yes, that would be my criterion — no wind. I can't believe how easy gardening would be. I'd even forfeit the view in exchange for shelter. Just now, the ice in the marsh is a jade colour flushed with an emerald green, and swirls of ice, the colour of milk, edge the islands. The colours are always changing, always extraordinary; sometimes they make me weep.

I think the name of the fish food is marvellous. Swimmy Baby. What with water in the basement, no leaf mould and runny marmalade, I'd quite like some myself right now, especially if it would make me "brighter and attractive."

Have you read the story by Gabrielle Roy, *Garden in the Wind*? It's in a book of short stories by the same name. I love it. It's about an elderly couple living on the prairies and they haven't spoken to each other in years. The husband is scornful of his wife growing flowers and going to such lengths to protect them from the cold and wind; she covers each blossom with a paper cone. She is dying and worries that the flowers will be killed by the first frost. She manages to get to the window and sees that her husband has put paper cones on all her flowers. This too makes me weep. I often think of this story when everything in the garden is being buffeted. I don't know where the book went but I think I gave it to someone going on a journey. Another book I can't find is Katherine White's *Onward and Upward in the Garden*. It must be somewhere in this house, but where?

You mention digging the pond at the farm. How? Manual labour?

Last summer I had a leopard frog in the garden; it's like a designer frog, more suited to Vancouver than New Brunswick. I hear a lot about the decline in amphibians and I don't remember hearing the peepers last spring. Maybe it's cyclical.

At last the marmalade is thickening and Tom just shouted up to me that it tastes like "Dundee." I won't need Swimmy Baby after all.

Love, Judy

 Water Lane
West Vancouver, B.C.
February 26

DEAR JUDY,
I'm enclosing *Onward and Upward in the Garden*, which I found in a second-hand book store some time ago and couldn't resist, although I already had a copy. I've read Gabrielle Roy's story *Garden in the Wind* and, strangely enough, I seem to remember reading it on a journey. Oops!

I've searched among my books in vain, so I'm afraid its fate remains a mystery.

Compared with the pond here, the one at the farm was a lake. It was chest-deep and far too big to have dug by hand. The ground was pure clay and we were lucky the back hoe didn't bog down. The children were still quite small and they had a wonderful time before the excavation filled with water. By tramping on the clay bottom, they could turn it into a sort of quaking jelly. It was quite a mess and so were they, but I really believe children need some mud in their lives. Plenty of mud round here right now — the spring rains are with us.

I never saw a leopard frog in New Brunswick and now it seems I might never see one anywhere. Recently the government of Alberta put out a *Have You Seen This Frog?* poster campaign hoping to solve the mystery of the vanishing northern leopard frog. Did you know how honoured you were to have one in your garden?

We do have one frog in this garden. It's vivid green with a white belly and a lurid red mouth. And it squeaks when you squeeze its belly. Julie's little girl gave it to me (Julie is a friend I met at the office). Whenever they visit, I try to hide the creature in a different place, but my game of hunt-the-frog took a strange turn when the local raccoon tribe joined in. They come pillaging most nights and have taken to sniffing out the hapless frog. They toss it about a bit, then lob it into the pond, and there it floats like a pallid corpse until I fish it out with a stick and hide it again. They're cheeky, these suburban raccoons. Did I tell you that I found one in our hallway

126

once? A muddy dishevelled ruffian. I wouldn't have minded so much if I hadn't just washed the tile floor. Moses, thank goodness, stays clear of them now but he learned the hard way, and not before the local vets had added him to their Christmas card list.

The die is cast! I mailed my seed order yesterday. I'm not sure if the selection process was a joy or an agony. Remember how it felt to spend your whole week's pocket money on a chocolate bar... or liquorice... or peppermints?

My first list, headed WANTS, two pages long, started with *Alliums* and *Anemones*, went on to *Bellis* and *Bergenias*, and romped along to S, where it ground to a halt because I couldn't pick out even two or three *Salvias* from so many tempting varieties. On my next attempt I nearly made it through the alphabet but stuck at wallflowers. Have you noticed that seed catalogues tend to list some things by the botanical name and some by the common name? It's maddening but, in the case of wallflowers, I forgive them. I don't know if the pundits have decided, once and for all, what the correct names are, but at this point I'm so confused I'm happy to settle for plain old wallflowers and the heck with *Chieranthus* and *Erysimum* and such.

After that, my list lay around the house for a few days and when I read it again I could hardly believe it was in my own handwriting. What could have possessed me? Where did I imagine I would put two types of *Verbascum* that grow to almost two metres and need full sun? Why did I want a two-tone pansy or a collector's cactus? On the other hand, how could I have missed the invaluable *Nicotiana langsdorffii*?

My second list, MUST HAVES, was heavily weighted in favour of annuals as I'd just read Wayne Winterrowd's beautifully written *Annuals for Connoisseurs* and knew I had to have every plant in the book. My third and final list, ABSOLUTE ESSENTIALS, was better balanced and was whittled down to a reasonable length (at least it fit onto the order form), though I never did manage to get rid of the splendid *Malva sylvestris ssp. mauritiana* 'Bibor Felho'. Thank goodness!

Bibor looks like a large, royal purple hollyhock but doesn't suffer from the rust that plagues hollyhocks. I saw him last summer on a tour of gardens in the Vancouver area, and was bowled over. I've no idea where I'm going to find room for such a huge sun lover but am prepared to deal with that problem later.

First I have to find a place to start the seeds. My greenhouse is still on paper and likely to stay that way for some time, but I'll start out on windowsills and then I'll probably expand into temporary cold frames on the deck.

My major indulgence was a packet of twenty hand-pollinated delphinium seeds. I'm not even going to tell you what they cost because you'll think the Pacific air has softened my brain. On the whole I'm proud of my restraint, which I admit was partly due to the knowledge that thirty more packets of seed are winging their way from England with the Royal Horticultural Society's free seed distribution. The deck may be a little crowded this spring but that'll be fine as long as I leave narrow paths to the door and to Ray's chair.

The volunteer seed collectors at VanDusen Botanical Gardens have their seeds available already. Let me know if you'd like any of them. Their list is enclosed. I'm also sending a packet of their valerian for you to have another try.

I don't think I told you about the garden tour I went on last summer (when I first met Bibor). It wasn't really a tour but an open-garden weekend. The ticket was a list of addresses with brief descriptions of the gardens, and participants visited as many as they wanted to. It's a wonderful idea and I marvel at the generosity of owners who open their gardens to crowds of people — the connoisseurs, the critics and the common or garden curious.

My own experiences with garden visitors have been bad, to say the least. Once in New Brunswick, when I gave a talk on perennials to a garden club, I illustrated it with slides of the garden at the farm. A few months later, to my horror, a carload of garden clubbers arrived on our doorstep "to admire the lovely perennials." By now, we were half way through a devastatingly hot August and our well had run dry. The new lawn, sodded rather late in the spring, looked like a scattering of large cornflakes and the only plants in flower, some annuals, had been flattened by a wind storm the week before.

Even worse was the time a client (I'll just call her Elizabeth Smith) came to examine my shrub roses. In those days, our overweight Welsh ponies, Dylan and Betty, were free to roam around the place. They were usually well behaved but when Betty sauntered round the corner of the house and bumped into a large and startled stranger, it spooked her badly and she charged into one end of the border while Elizabeth Smith staggered back into the other. "Betty," I yelled, "get out of there, you fat fool!" I knew the visit had gone badly but I didn't know how badly until some time later when I heard my ex-client referred to as Betty Smith.

I don't think I'll be opening this garden to the public in a hurry.

Love, Elspeth

P.S. Oh dear! As soon as the order was sent, I should have put the catalogue away. I just flipped it open and remembered with a dreadful pang that the *Unique formula blending of selected Toad lily Hybrids Mixed, which thrive in dappled shade, are easy to grow and long lived,* was expunged — expunged!

 Kennebecasis River Road
Hampton, N.B.
March 3

DEAR ELSPETH,
Scant snow cover and bitter cold. Every driveway is sheer ice and all I can hear is the sound of tires trying to get traction. I slipped on the front path and crashed onto my hip. What a bruise! I should have been watching my step but instead I was looking at a rose bush standing in a block of ice. I tried to dig it out last year because it was getting too big for the spot it was in. The job was much harder than I thought so I gave up and never got back to the hole. I wouldn't really mind if this particular rose didn't survive, but I suspect that nothing will daunt it, not even the Scotch Gardener.

One rose I hope survives is Harrison's Yellow. It is supposed to be the *Yellow Rose of Texas* and because our boys were born there I've always been partial to things Texan. I planted it last spring and towards the end of June noted in my diary: Harrison's Yellow came out today. Two weeks later I wrote: Harrison's Yellow died today. Tiny caterpillars had eaten every leaf, every single leaf. I looked in *Roses for Canadian Gardens* — I got the rose from Corn Hill — and saw that the caterpillar is the larval stage of the sawfly and the way to get rid of them is to kick the bush or knock it with a padded stick — I felt like using a blunt instrument. Anyway, I cut the bush back somewhat and in the fall it was leafing out quite nicely. I smothered it with hay and am hoping for the best.

Next to the rose in the block of ice is a plant I *wouldn't* mind getting rid of — *Physosteiga*. I call it physiotherapist. Its common name is Obedient Plant but it's not at all obedient; it has spread like crazy and flops all over the place. Sophie has it growing between wild rose bushes so it can't flop around, but of course, I'm trying to get *rid* of the rose bush. With this weather and my sore hip I'm glad I'm off to California in two weeks to stay with some old friends, Marge and Henry. I looked into the fare to Vancouver but it was still high. I was looking forward to seeing you in your new setting, but there will no doubt be another time.

It must be thirty years since I lived in Los Angeles. I got a job that included my fare being paid from London to California. When I look back it seems like a different life.

I had always wanted to go to California because of a lesson I had in school. The teacher discussed world climates. He dismissed Canada by thumping the map hanging on the wall and saying "Cold. Cold. Cold." Then he alighted in California. I can remember his exact words: "In California, you can plan a picnic six weeks ahead and know the weather will be perfect." As an eleven-year-old living in Wales, where the weather changed every minute, I found this hard to believe, but was impressed, so impressed that my one aim in life was to go there and see if it was true. And it was.

Shortly after I arrived in Los Angeles, Marge (who also arrived from England at the same time) and I were asked out to dinner. "Come at six-thirty and we'll eat at seven." We arrived at the proper time but the hostess seemed surprised to see us and greeted us in a slightly distraught way. She was wearing clothes that made her look like a court jester; jingling and striped was the impression I had. There was no husband around, and I think he was the one that really invited us because I seem to remember he said his grandmother came from Wales. There was also no food in evidence. She gave us drinks and more drinks. There was fractured chat and then she said she had to pop out to the store. By nine she was still not back, and my God, we'd had so much liquor by then and on empty stomachs…

I said to Marge, "Let's raid the garden and search for food." I hoped for the odd carrot or pea. There were tall flowers growing against a trellis; I wasn't a gardener in those days and asked Marge what they were. She said, "Hollywocks." "Hollywocks?" I said, and we were both convulsed with laughter. We laughed so hard we nearly fell into the pool. I've not thought of that in years and was wondering if we ever got any food at all and why it was all so mysterious. I must ask Marge about it. I'd like to have some hollyhocks, maybe up against the fence David and I built.

Thanks for the seed order from VanDusen. What about a couple of hollyhocks?

Verbascum is mullein, isn't it? The first fall we spent in Canada, I saw the rosettes of mullein growing in a field and was so taken with them I dug them up, potted them and had them as house plants. What I would like, though, is the *Mecanopsis* Blue Poppy. I have an illustration of it in *Great Gardens of Britain*. What an amazing blue, but I don't suppose it would survive here. Bibor Felho sounds magnificent, but it too would never survive.

Oh, yes. Thanks also for *Onward and Upward*. It is nice to have again.

I'll miss the bird feeder while I'm away. This morning we must have had about fifty evening grosbeaks squawking and fighting out there, when suddenly into their midst flew a mourning dove. She alighted on the feeder and the grosbeaks were instantly silenced; they froze and stared at her but didn't fly away. She looked very dignified turning her head slowly from side to side watching them. It was as though a maiden aunt had come to tea. She said grace and they very quietly resumed their feeding. I couldn't get over the difference in their behaviour. One of them close to her got a bit rambunctious, so she gave him a little peck.

Love, Judy

Water Lane
West Vancouver, B.C.
March 18

DEAR JUDY,
I do wish you were coming to Vancouver. Ah well, I know
you'll have a wonderful time in California, though it's still a
bit early for hollywocks. I certainly hope Marge can
remember what happened to your jingling hostess because
you can't leave me cliff-hanging like this. If both of you were
too far gone to remember what *really* happened, then feel
free to make something up!

I've often had a good laugh over plant names, and not
necessarily on an empty stomach either. So much garden lore
is passed by word of mouth it's easy to understand how a
lemon balm, for instance, can turn into a lemon bomb.

One of my clients once pointed to her *Epimediums* and
told me how much she liked happy mediums. I agreed. I
thought it was the perfect name for a plant that would never
give offense to anyone. It was harder to keep a straight face
when a fellow with very decided opinions started laying
down the law to me about his macho pines and wigglers. I'd
have guessed *Mugo* for macho but without the shrub in front
of me I'd never have recognised the *Weigela*. Another time
he told me he disliked anonymous bushes; I've also heard the
Euonymus called humungous.

You must know of popples in New Brunswick, for poplars,
and cotoneaster is often cotton Easter. Even the gardening
British have given up on some botanical names. *Alstromeria*
sounds friendlier as Ulster Mary anyway, and it was only
common sense to rechristen the *Mlokosewitschii* peony,

Molly the witch.

Plant name pronunciation is a sort of occupational hazard in gardening. I blush to think how often, in all innocence, I pronounced Pinus to rhyme with Venus. While for genus (which should have rhymed with Venus) I said genus (to rhyme with Venice). Here in Vancouver a great debate rages over CLEMatis and cleMATis. I try to stick to local pronunciations but this one has me so confused I can't even remember which way I say it myself.

When I first started speaking in public I used to worry about these pitfalls but now I'm more relaxed. I was told that the best way to cope with a word you couldn't pronounce was to say it loudly. This is the *if in doubt, shout!* principle, familiar to politicians. And, after all, it doesn't matter a hoot how something's said as long as it's clear to everyone which plant you're talking about.

I can almost see your ladylike mourning dove; she's wearing an elegantly simple jersey wool dress in a discreet shade of beige, and a lorgnette perhaps? Each day it seems there are more birds in this garden and I'm getting better at recognising them. The Steller's jays are easy; they're dark iridescent blue with black heads, quite unlike the eastern jays but just as raucous. Today there's a varied thrush scuffling about under the roses; it's like a robin with extra decoration. I noticed that the odd hummingbird stayed around right through the winter, and if it weren't for Moses, I'd put up a feeder for them.

Last year, when we moved in, a pair of mallard ducks was visiting the pond every day. After a few weeks, they stopped coming and as usual I blamed Moses. A few days ago, they reappeared and are now regular visitors again, so maybe they just spend their spring holidays here and maybe Moses is as innocent as he'd have me believe. They make a handsome addition to the garden scene. She forages non-stop among the water lily debris and he sits on guard looking gorgeous. I've never seen him eat a single morsel.

Instead of the ospreys we used to see at the farm, we have bald eagles. They circle the park and sometimes perch on a dead tree across the road. For such big birds their cries are pathetic — like sick hens. When Jean went to Whistler on the train recently, she saw a vast colony of them roosting in the trees; she gave up counting after eighty. It's good to know there's such a healthy population around.

I was standing in the driveway the other day when one flew past me, heading down the road. It gave me quite a shock; after all, these things have a two-metre wing span and at eye level their beaks look alarmingly fierce. Later on I heard the sequel to the story. The children who live next door to Anne had called her over to see something in their front garden. It was an eagle lying — well, spreadeagled —

on the ground. They watched it for several minutes and, thinking it was injured, were about to dial 911 for help, when it suddenly shook itself and took off, revealing a second eagle underneath. I suppose these birds are designed for soaring flight, not aerial acrobatics, but I don't know why these two chose such a public spot for their earthbound nuptials.

I hope the bruise is better and that California will be splendid.

Love, Elspeth

California
March 25

It is far more lush than I remember, perhaps on account of unusually heavy rain this spring. California poppies everywhere, purple, yellow and white daisies, and hillsides magenta with ice plants. I wish I'd been a gardener when I lived here, but at 22 you have other things on your mind. I'm sitting in the garden — no flies or mosquitoes. I've just eaten an avocado right off the tree. Oh how I love them. I've been weeding and digging around an orange tree. Did you just get a whiff of the orange blossom? And the warmth. I can hardly believe it.

JAM

Kennebecasis River Road
Hampton, N.B.
April 5

DEAR ELSPETH,
Boy, was it cold when I got back from California, but even
though it was midnight I couldn't wait to see if anything was
growing in the garden. I crept around with a flashlight,
feeling like a burglar stealing garden gnomes. I ran my hands
over tulip bulbs a few centimetres high, a Daphne was in
flower and William and Mary were just out, but the mulch
was still frozen to the ground.

In California we walked a lot, sometimes along the beach
but often just up the road to admire the gardens: hedges of
azaleas, arbours spilling over with
wisteria, lilies along the walkways.
One garden was taken over by the
most magnificent succulents and
cacti I've ever seen. I saw a chain
link fence covered with passion vine.
Its flowers are so decorative they
don't look natural, but then, what does
in California?

The orange trees impressed me. I've just read an article
describing how I can grow orange trees in Canada — in a
sun drenched living room or in a solarium. The young trees
are expensive, so by the time I've had a solarium built,
bought trees and fertilizer, and jacked the heat up in the
house, it would be cheaper to visit California. Why am I
bitching? I already have a mock orange.

I visited a friend's new house. A nice place, with lovely

tiled floors. The garden in the back was hedged with colourful firethorn, California lilac and azaleas, but in the middle was a huge mass of bricks, a sort of dais about knee-high with recessed lights. It took up most of the garden space. I couldn't make out what it was for and neither could anyone else. Funny isn't it, the ideas people have about what makes a garden.

I asked Marge about the "hollywock" affair. She said she'd told me but I couldn't remember. Apparently, the couple had split up and the wife, Velma, had moved out. When Velma knew her husband wouldn't be at home she'd sneak in and take as much stuff as she could — can you blame her? We turned up and she thought we were his latest playmates. Marge said we never got any food as husband didn't show, so we just left. I drove a yellow Ford in those days and as we were driving down the highway — in search of food — I kept saying, "There's a car right behind us, the exact same colour. It's really close. Someone's after us. Oh God, if he hits us we're in trouble." Neither of us was in good shape. "Pull over then, pull over," she kept saying, "I don't want to be repatriated!" I eventually pulled over. We looked through the back window and discovered that the yellow lid of the trunk had sprung up and that's what I thought was another car.

One of the highlights of the trip happened on the first day. Jonathan phoned from San Diego on his way back up the coast. They were docking there for a few nights. So, armed with a large assortment of food, we all went down to see him. After five months at sea I wondered if the crew would still be talking to one another, but they were. It was so good to see him and Maria, his girlfriend, who was the only other one I knew. What a coincidence that I should be in California at the same time! The closest I'll come to my life imitating a movie.

It's been hard getting back to real life after two weeks of glorious sunshine. Last night I really knew I was back; the fields were burning. I don't know why people around here do this, but they say it makes the grass grow. Have you ever known grass not to? Maybe they burn the fields for the same reason Shetlanders plan a jamboree to set a boat alight. It was eerie seeing the fields necklaced with flames. If they'd just stick to grass, but often garages and houses go up in smoke.

Today it was a bit warmer so I spent time in the garden shed. I started out in full winter plumage but as the temperature rose, I threw off layers — very thin layers.

I was starting seeds in margarine tubs. Mixing my own potting soil with peat moss and vermiculite reminded me of mixing up mash for chickens when I was a kid. I hated chickens. Whenever I opened the chicken house door, they flew at me and would have liked to peck my eyes out.

I was given seeds of Siberian wallflower. Is it a strict perennial — as opposed to a lenient one — or does it reseed itself? I like a plant with "Siberian" in its name. I feel more assured about its performance. I bet the magnificent Bibor Felho would survive if it was Siberian Felho. I wish I had Siberia in my own name.

Taking the containers of seeds from the shed into the house to germinate was like running the gauntlet. I walked with my back to the wind, bent over the trays of seeds to shelter them. I felt like a crab. One year the wind scooped the earth neatly out of my little pots. Inside the house I put them above the fridge and covered them with plastic. I look

at them a million times a day, although I don't expect
germination in a hurry or at all really. It still amazes me that
a tomato will grow from one small seed and a wallflower
from another, and they never get mixed up! You never see a
tomato with a wallflower blossom, and you can explain it
biologically until you are blue in the face, and I will still be
amazed.

Once they're on their way, I'll put them back in the shed. I
have a heat lamp in there. It gives off a warm red glow and
neighbours have said they like to see it when they drive
home late at night or, on the other hand, wonder what the
hell's going on in there.

Love, Ms. Siberia

 Water Lane
West Vancouver, B.C.
April 22

DEAR JUDY,
I've never been to California but you make it sound
tempting. We've had steady rain for weeks here and I'm sick
of grey skies. Everyone talks of growing webbed feet.

California lilacs survive in this area but we're on the
northern edge of their range so they need a favourable spot.
I'd love to plant some but my favourable spots are all
earmarked for other goodies, including another Californian,
Carpenteria californica, which I'm planning to grow against
the south-facing wall of the office. I already have a lemon

tree though. Sort of. Eric, a young Scot who worked at the office, grew it from a pip and nurtured it with loving care. When he left to go travelling in South America he entrusted it to me. I felt quite honoured. I have it in the living room window and it's suffering from lack of sunshine (aren't we all?) but I'm hoping it'll pick up in the summer when I put it on the deck. The blossom smells wonderful in the evenings but Ray finds it overpowering and has been nipping the flowers off. Eric would approve; he only let it carry one lemon at a time. I notice, however, that three small green fruits have slipped past the flower police and are swelling rapidly.

Mixing potting soil has often made me think of baking, but never of chicken mash, although we did have hens when I was a child. I remember watching my mother cook up quantities of smelly hen food in a large steel pressure cooker with hefty clamps and a dial on the lid. It looked more like a weapon of war than a household utensil and I was always in awe of it. With good reason. It hissed horribly and was inclined to explode.

I grew up thinking hens were a normal part of the suburban garden. I'm sure it's against the local bylaws here to keep farmyard animals but I know of two families who keep a few feathered pets with the neighbours' blessings. Which reminds me; I think the local bylaws also forbid clotheslines in gardens and, if it's true, I should really do something about it.

I have a seeding tip to pass on to you. There is so little insulation in most fridges, the top stays cold in spite of the heat rising from the back. Instead of standing the seed pots directly on the surface, try putting them on a tea tray placed upside down and overhanging the back of the fridge. This way the tray scoops the warm air in under the pots. The sushi we had at Rob and Kimi's wedding reception was delivered on polystyrene trays which sag a bit but do the job nicely.

There are plenty of ways to make seeding seem difficult. For instance you can soak the seeds in a dilute solution of seaweed before planting them. (I don't, because wet seeds stick together and are hard to sow evenly). Or you can make sure the seeds are all aligned north-south. I'm serious. In research between 1957 and 1960, Urban Pittman of Alberta found that seeds lined up this way began to grow eight or twelve hours earlier than their fellows; apparently something to do with the earth's magnetic field. Fascinating, but I'm not about to get out the tweezers and buy a microscope. Like you, I don't expect germination in a hurry. It's like having babies and raising a family — think about it too much and you'd never get started. There's so much to know and so much to go wrong that, sooner or later, you simply have to put the books aside, ignore the helpful advice and just *do* it.

Years ago, when I was making up my first soil mix for seeds, I added a bucketful of sawdust. Goodness knows why. It was just another of those little incidents that get filed away in every gardener's brain as *it seemed a bright idea at the time*. The result was disastrous but of course I learned something from the experience. As Oscar Wilde said, "Experience is the name everyone gives to their mistakes."

By the way, in answer to your question, Siberian wallflower is usually grown as a biennial and will probably seed itself in the garden if you remember not to weed out the offspring. I've had plants, however, that wintered over a second time,

144

and other plants that seemed reluctant to seed themselves at all; just another reminder that gardening isn't the exact science we expect it to be when we start out.

Professional work is going well and work on the office extension at the front of the house starts next week. It'll be quite an upheaval as all the office equipment will be moved temporarily into the dining room and the living room will become a bedroom. Footing drains have to be installed and connected to the storm sewer. Needless to say this means trenching. Luckily the line will run down the side of the pond and, as it's impossible to get a machine in there, Ray is doing the job by hand. I have to move everything in his path but I don't mind because the place is so thick with weeds it needs to be completely cleaned out anyway.

The new path around the pond will run between planting beds as it does now, but I'll exaggerate the curves so it comes right up to the water in places then swings away to make room for larger plantings between water and path. A low wall and my new border of shrubs already screen the pond garden from the driveway and from the entry. Along the property line, I'll thicken up the planting to make a dense wall of evergreens, and at the bottom end, when I've brought up the level, I'll plant more evergreens. This way the pond will be enclosed in a garden room with green walls winter and summer, and I can decorate the interior with herbaceous perennials and small deciduous trees and shrubs.

I can see it so clearly in my mind's eye, it's quite a shock to look out and see nothing there but mud and rocks.

The greenhouse will be a lean-to outside the kitchen window. I'll be able to look through it to the pond while I do the dishes. Even with eastern exposure we'll make sure it has enough roof vents. Overheating can be a real headache in greenhouses.

Did I ever tell you about Moses and the greenhouse at the farm?

We had roof vents which opened and closed automatically, controlled by a thermostat. Fly screens were fitted below the opening lights and Moses soon discovered that they made the perfect spot for sunning. Ah, the bliss of stretching full length, bathed in upward currents of tropical air! I was working in the greenhouse one evening when something above me caught my eye. Silhouetted against the sky it looked like a large ink blot. Or like a cartoon cat flattened in the wake of a road roller. Poor Moses had slept so soundly, the closing vent had trapped him, squeezed between the glass and the bulging screen.

I was so frantic, I couldn't think which way to spin the thermostat. It seemed an age before the vents creaked open and slowly, like bread dough rising, Moses was restored to three dimensions. He stalked off with only a slight stagger and, for the sake of his pride, I didn't start laughing until he was out of earshot.

Love, Elspeth

Kennebecasis River Road
Hampton, N.B.
May 5

DEAR ELSPETH,

I really hate to ask this but where on earth are you going to plant all the seedlings you've started? Or haven't you faced that question? You say you have a local bylaw that prohibits clotheslines. No good me living out there, as it's the only domestic chore I like. The trouble is, I go out to put the clothes on the line and don't come back in for hours. I find I can slave in the garden from dawn to dusk, but in the house I'm overcome with exhaustion just plugging in the vacuum cleaner.

The frost has left the ground and I can dig over the vegetable patch. I pulled the mulch off a few weeks ago to expose the earth and let it warm up; a nice job that, like baring your flesh to the sun. Pulling the mulch off is one of the first rites of spring; no more shovelling snow and slipping on ice. It's the beginning of a brand new gardening year which will be very different from every other year, because *this* is the year when *everything* will miraculously come together.

As you know, I love digging. The spade sinking into the soil is like slicing through Black Forest cake, a piece of which I wouldn't mind right now. Last year I helped a friend dig some of his potatoes. The earth in that garden had been treated to large amounts of mushroom compost and was perfect. I just nudged the fork under the plant and then got into the earth with my hands. It was so finely textured and so warm. Mine isn't like that.

I think I may plant some potatoes myself this year. When we first moved to this house I put some in, but they were covered with scab and attracted hordes of potato bug. Seeing the striped bugs on the leaves gave me quite a start because I was just a little kid when I last came across them. It was during the war and because my father was the local constable we lived in the police station. On the office wall was a poster covered with large pictures of colourful beetles. I used to sit on the table, swinging my legs and staring endlessly at it. I think I learned to read from this poster. It said if you saw the Colorado beetle it was your duty to report it. I grew up thinking the Colorado beetle was the enemy.

So I have this sort of affinity with potato beetles and hate to squash them. That's partly why I haven't planted any potatoes since. But I have missed eating the small ones with butter.

When I start out in spring I always wear work gloves and vow I shall wear them all through the season. It's the small thorns and tiny cuts that are so uncomfortable. But soon, I'm taking off one glove to pull out a weed, then the other to transplant a seedling, and of course I never find them again until after a good rain. I had a pair of gloves once that even when left out in a deluge never got wet, but when I was wearing them, my hands got soaked. They were made completely out of synthetic materials.

After digging the vegetable garden I raked it over. It looked so smooth and tidy I thought it a shame to disturb it with plants. Each year it's the same; I stand and admire the pristine ground and one year I know, I shall admire it so long I'll completely miss the planting season.

But enough admiration! I had to get manure. I went to the

local vet's, filled buckets and put them in the back of the car. This is another covert operation. Tom isn't keen on manure in the car even though I put newspaper all over the back and am very careful. Back in the garden I spread the manure. Later, my beloved came out of the house and said, "Can you smell anything?" I sniffed the air and said, "It's the pulp mill."

I have a couple of rum barrels which I use to collect rain from the roof. I turned these upright and rolled them into place. When I first bought them the smell of rum was so strong I thought of opening up a little bar. The vegetables I grew that year were so merry I could have used a Vegetation Supervisor.

The chimney swifts are back. Each year they return to nest in the chimney that runs through our bedroom. I love watching them turn and twist and drop down into the chimney; they seem to hang in the air then finally drop down. In bed, I can hear them spiralling around in there. When the young start to feed they make an awful din all through the night. I often wonder how they learn to fly, stuck in the chimney all the time, and where did they nest before chimneys?

Another species to appear in spring are pairs of women walking down our street. I think they all hope to shed pounds of flesh by walking it off. Some of them fling their arms back and forth like windmills — it's a wonder they don't knock each other's eyes out. Others lumber along. One I saw was dressed in black tight pants and black shoes and walked with slightly splayed feet, but the way she held her arms reminded me of a seal; another walks with such a strange gait she looks as though she's wading through water.

But seeing them emerge is a good sign that winter is past.

Throughout the winter I've collected bags of sawdust for the paths. I had them lined up in the garden. They looked very inviting, like bean bags, so I sank down into one of them. As I sank, a stream of sawdust shot out through a small hole in the plastic: sawdust everywhere, hair, eyelashes, clothes.

Love, Judy

P.S. I remembered what happened to poor Moses, but I still laughed when I read your last letter.

 Water Lane
West Vancouver, B.C.
May 29

DEAR JUDY,
Construction is underway. It makes me nervous to see shingles flying off the roof, and scaffolding standing in the rose bank. Our builders are doing their best to avoid garden casualties. Heaven knows, I've warned them about it often enough. The wonder is they haven't thrown me off the roof as well.

The office extension will help to enclose a small entry area which I'm planning to pave. Already, in my mind, it's The Courtyard. I've always loved the notion of a courtyard — it sounds so established. The greenhouse will eventually form the back wall of this area, with access from the deck. I know

I keep mentioning this greenhouse, but it's important to me. I've always thought of a greenhouse as a place apart, like a small foreign country you can step into for a brief holiday.

In the greenhouse at the farm, vegetable seedlings and tomatoes had priority, but here I had a more ornamental set-up in mind. Ray, however, had his own ideas and suddenly took it upon himself to clear a space for a vegetable plot along the back fence next to Anne's. There goes THE PLAN! Remember — work from the front to the back?

Since we moved here, I've really missed a steady supply of our own organically grown vegetables, though I admit it was a relief, last summer, not to have buckets of green beans and zucchinis to deal with every second day. I haven't come to terms with *buying* green beans yet — limp ones at that. Still, it was a surprise to find that Ray felt even more strongly about home-grown produce than I did.

Anyway, I'm delighted to be back in the vegetable business. There's something absolutely right about growing and eating your own food. There are brave attempts in the Vancouver area to encourage allotments and city farming and although they aren't exactly a mainstream part of city life (any more than gardening is part of today's school curricula) they are evidently having some effect. Jean, who has found an apartment in the downtown area, told me the other day she wanted a worm composter for her balcony garden. There's hope for the environment yet!

It's a bonus for us that the previous owners here were keen on fruit. There were apples, cherries, plums and a pear as well as a fig tree, kiwi vines and raspberry canes. There was even a hop scrambling through the bushes by the entry but I took it out. I felt if I didn't get it first, it would get me. I feel that way about the kiwis too; I've never seen anything grow so far, so fast, and the stems are like boa constrictors.

One of the few, very few, plants missing from this garden was rhubarb, but Julie gave me a good chunk of root which is doing so well I've already picked a few stalks.

Ellen stayed with us last week on her way back to the Island (she sends her love) and while she was here, made a deliciously moist and sticky rhubarb coffee-cake. The recipe is:

1 1/2 cups brown sugar
2 1/2 cups flour (I'd substitute whole wheat)
1 tsp. salt
l tsp. baking soda
2 cups (at least) raw chopped rhubarb
1/2 cup walnuts (broken or roughly chopped)
1 egg
1 cup milk
2/3 cup oil
Mix, spread in pan and sprinkle on a topping of:
1/4 cup butter
1/2 cup sugar
1/2 cup sliced almonds
(I found this topping too sticky to work with so I added a handful of flour to make a more crumbly mix. And next time I'll use butter straight from the fridge and cut it into the sugar with a fork or a pastry blender.)
Bake in a 325°F oven for an hour.

Have you heard the old rhyming recipe for rhubarb punch?

One of sour, one of sweet, two of strong, and drink it neat.
The sour is rhubarb juice, the sweet, maple syrup, and the
strong, rum. It might be just the thing to go with your
imaginary Black Forest cake.

Oh no, I've just remembered — you hate rhubarb!

Apart from the new vegetable patch, we've stuck to our
resolve and turned a blind eye on the chaos of the jungle.
The growth in there is frightening. Below the pond garden,
I've done nothing, and the area which, last year, was a mere
tangle is this year a solid mass of greenery with two small
tunnels burrowing through it. The brambles are the worst
culprits. Now and then, Ray wades in and attacks them with
a machete but what he really needs is a tank. Or that big
back hoe again.

We have a young friend staying with us from the Shetland
Islands. She seemed keen to explore the garden and I walked
around the pond with her, then pointed out one of the
tunnel entrances. She looked a little nervous, which was
quite out of character, and stood hesitating at the mouth.
Finally she asked innocently, "Do you have a map?" I'd have
suggested a trail of breadcrumbs but I knew the slugs would
get them long before she found her way back to civilisation.

In spite of our cramped quarters, I'm enjoying working on
garden design again. The profession of landscape architec-
ture includes everything from environmental assessment on
a vast scale to helping a beginner gardener plan a perennial
border. I prefer the small-scale end of things; it gives me a
better chance to work creatively with plants as well as with
hard materials and I like its ongoing nature. I was involved in
one garden in New Brunswick for twenty years. I also like
the contact with people.

I've often thought my job is not so much the creation of gardens as the creation of gardeners. After all, you can't have a real garden without real involvement by somebody. Maybe that's why I've started teaching garden design at night school classes. I team teach with Julie; it's much more fun than working solo and she is wonderfully well organised. When my enthusiasms get out of hand, she tactfully steers me back to our lesson plan. I have another friend, Doreen, an ex-teacher, who's been giving us helpful tips about teaching techniques.

I like designing with people who will do at least some of the work themselves and, even if a landscape contractor is to be involved, I encourage owners to put in some of their own new plants; it gives them a proprietary interest they'd never have otherwise. The most successful gardens don't turn into show places overnight, and often don't turn into show places ever. But they do make a big difference to somebody's life.

Well, what a lecture! It's time I did some cleaning but, before I do, I'll tell you about my latest haircut.

Hairdressing establishments always make me feel like a country bumpkin. I think it's the mirrors and my gardener's fingernails that do it. Usually I try to act cool, sit on my hands and keep quiet but, this time, the assistant was sweeping up piles of hair clippings and the longer I watched, the more I thought what a waste it was to throw them out, and the more I knew I was going to open my mouth and say something unsophisticated.

"Oooh, lovely stuff!" I blurted out. "Great for the garden."

Amazingly, my blonde hairdresser took this in her stride. I could have hugged her.

"Want some?" she asked. "It'll make good compost." Then,

after clipping in silence for some time, she added, "Especially yours." More clipping while I mulled this over.

Finally I had to ask, "You mean red hair makes better compost?"

"Not red," she said, "virgin."

"Virgin hair?"

Now I know some composters take their art very seriously. I've even heard of people who compost their cast-off clothing. But sorcery is something else again. I wondered what your Scotch Gardener would make of it.

I was on the point of confessing to three children and a healthy husband but — to cut a long story short enough for me to vacuum up today's plaster dust before I run out of energy — it turns out that very few people round here have hair which is neither coloured nor curled artificially. Strange, isn't it? I'd never thought of my own hair as organically grown produce.

Love, Elspeth

 Kennebecasis River Road
Hampton, N.B.
June 7

DEAR MS. VIRGIN HAIR,
What a strange term. Yes, I would have thought it applied only to virgins — they too are pretty rare. What about virgin wool and extra-virgin olive oil? Since you mentioned it I keep thinking of "the virgin sturgeon needs no urgin'."

I've been in the vegetable patch planting scarlet runners, using beans I saved from last year's crop. If I put a plastic flower pot over each one, I find they germinate quicker and seem to escape the slugs and it's nice to see the emerging bean push up the pot. I think I've used every method known to man to hold them up, but now I'm back to my original method of bamboo beanpoles. I was in the hardware store and overheard an old gardener telling another man that he used bamboo beanpoles and had his peas and beans use the same poles; after the peas had finished with them the beans took over. I lean mine together in pairs and tie a pole along the top and hope they stay that way. When I was sixteen or seventeen I went to France for a summer and lived with a family in the country. We ate every meal outside under the trees and often had scarlet runners for dinner, alone on the plate with butter. Sounds poignant, doesn't it... *alone on the plate with butter*? But the taste was superb and I've been trying to recapture it ever since. I think now I like the memory of them more than the beans themselves.

While I was tying up beanpoles I kept getting a whiff of the lilac bushes. The smell of lilacs always takes me back to when I was a little kid. I must have told you about it, haven't I? In case I haven't, I will. I can even remember the coat I was wearing; it was a chocolate colour with a brown velvet collar and matching flaps on the pockets. The buttons were just like Malteasers. Anyway, my mother and sister and I got off the bus on a warm sunny day, and walked down a narrow lane, over a railway crossing, and into the farm yard of a friend of my mother's. There were new calves in the barn, and for tea we had shiny butter on brown bread that we cut up into soldiers and dipped into brown boiled eggs. I don't remember where the lilac bushes were on the farm or even their colour, but always the smell brings back this strong wonderful memory.

Wherever I've lived I've always had a lot of rhubarb around, but have never quite known what to do with it. When I put it in pies it sets my teeth on edge. But I must say the rhubarb coffee cake turned out a treat. I wish I'd had the recipe years ago. My sister and I often visited an aunt who grew rhubarb and insisted we take bundles of it home to my mother. We hated it. So, going home on the train, we opened the window and hurled the rhubarb out stick by stick. I can still see it flying through the air.

I seem to have had an attack of nostalgia. Must be the rhubarb.

Courtyards appeal to me in a big way, as they do to you. In New Orleans I fell in love with them — elegant windows looking out over balconies with wrought iron railings, and geraniums everywhere. For me, the height of luxury would be a bedroom opening through French doors onto a very private courtyard so that first thing in the morning I could throw the doors open and step outside. I'd have a tiled floor and small apricot trees espaliered on the walls, even though espalier makes me uneasy. There'd be orange trees in terracotta pots and wicker furniture. The bedroom would have a fireplace and I'd wrap myself in a large white towel warmed against the fire.

It's time I stopped dreaming and went out into the garden. I don't think I'll be bothering with broccoli this year — I've never managed to keep the damned caterpillars out of it. One time, a friend came to supper, and I saw her pop a caterpillar into her mouth along with the broccoli; another

time a visitor hid them under his fork. So this year I think I'll
give it a miss. There is so much to do at this time of year
when winter runs straight into summer and everything
happens at once. The grass needs cutting, the edges need
trimming, the annuals have to be planted out and as usual
everything needs tying up. At least there's no shortage of lath
for staking; it's one of the few advantages of living in an old
house constantly in need of renovation.

I know just what you mean about stepping into a
greenhouse. I love going into glass houses in botanical
gardens, especially in winter. The warmth and scent strips
reality away. But you still haven't said where you will plant all
the new seedlings. You could set up a stall in the market.

Love, Judy

 Water Lane
West Vancouver, B.C.
June 18

DEAR JUDY,
What a nag you are! I don't know why you keep asking where
all my seedlings will go when there's obviously room
somewhere. Ray's vegetable garden? Maybe not.

The driveway is clogged with heaps of lumber and broken
plaster board, the front part of the house has disappeared
under a vast blue tarpaulin, and the only way in or out is to
walk the plank across one of the trenches. But you know all
about this kind of thing so I won't go on about it. I'll go on

about my beloved Camperdown elm instead.

   It looked lovely when the leaves first came out but it kept shedding twigs and was soon looking a little weary. I checked out a few books, and this is what I read in Michael A. Dirr's *Manual of Woody Landscape Plants*:

> *The following list should provide an idea of the potential problems which may beset "your" elm.*

This was in reference to American elms, but Mr. Dirr sounded like a man who understood my new-found pride of possession so I read on eagerly.

> *Wetwood is a bacterial disease which appears as a wilt, branch dieback, and internal and external fluxing of elms. A pipe is often placed in the tree to relieve the tremendous gas pressure that builds up; no control known.*

Good grief!

There was worse to come. The list of potential problems was like a compendium of pestilence, from beetles, borers and blights through caligrapha, cockscombe gall and eight kinds of cankers to scorches and scales and, worst of all, Dutch elm disease. Did you know that arborists refer to it, ominously, as DED? DED spread to Eastern Canada from the States but the open spaces of the prairies have checked its westward spread — so far. The Camperdown is sometimes listed as a cross between Scotch and smooth-leaved elms and some varieties of smooth-leaved elms are resistant to DED. Is Crowley's tree still alive? If so, DED may be one less thing for

159

me to worry about.

There are plenty of others.

Aphids are supposed to be attracted to yellow, so a couple of weeks ago I hung up sticky yellow traps. They attracted leafhoppers and the mailman, but the aphids were too snug in their curled up leaves to bother with such nonsense. Hundreds of leafhoppers met a sticky end but thousands more escaped and flew out in suffocating clouds whenever the leaves were disturbed. When I discovered that a hose jet knocked them to the ground, I thought I'd made a breakthrough for organic pest control. I hadn't. They were only lying doggo till they dried off. Discouraging, but the scale was worse.

Mr. Dirr didn't include leafhoppers in his list of ghastly elm ailments, but he did mention scale. When I realised that these harmless-looking bumps, like small buds on every twig, were actually adult creatures hatching into hundreds of crawling scale-to-be, I almost wept. It's easy enough to scrape them off with a small sharp stone but I've been using up all my precious gardening time on one small tree, and our regular passers-by are starting to look at me strangely. Even Anne, I can tell, is having doubts.

And before you begin to have doubts as well, I'll switch from my pest problems to yours. Did you know that there's a fabric available to keep insects from laying eggs on plants such as broccoli? It's lightweight and porous so you can drape it over young transplants and leave it in place as they grow. It's fairly expensive, even if you reuse it a few times, and it doesn't look pretty, but it's an alternative to serving caterpillars, or pesticides, for dinner.

By the way, I'm so glad you still call them caterpillars; I

never completely came to terms with worms instead of caterpillars, or for that matter, with dirt for earth, yards for gardens or gardens for vegetables — as in "Got yer garden in, yet?" That's a phrase I haven't heard since we came out west; probably because it's normal to plant vegetables over an extended season here, not over one frantic weekend.

Love, Elspeth

Kennebecasis River Road
Hampton, N.B.
July 1

DEAR ELSPETH
Before I forget, I just drove by Crowley's and their Camperdown looks great, like a green-leaved umbrella, so maybe they won't get the dreaded Dutch elm. I don't think they pay much attention to it except for putting cement in it that one year. According to what you tell me about yours, their tree seems much smaller. I bet it's not troubled by blue aphids. We wouldn't have anything as exotic as that! Did I read somewhere that a nursery had come up with an elm resistant to Dutch elm?

And as for fabric to protect the broccoli, I don't think that would do it for mine because of the unceasing wind across my garden. I'd spend more time chasing after it than I would in the garden. Because of the wind, I've tried to concentrate on growing short plants, though looking around at the delphiniums, lilies, and phlox you wouldn't think so. Anyway, last year was the first time I grew the short gaillardia, the one with the dark red centre and yellow fringe. I think I must have dropped a packet of seeds in the garden the year before, because later on in summer I saw clumps of vegetation I couldn't identify — not unusual for me. So I thought to myself, It must be *something*. I separated the clumps and planted them in different parts of the garden, on the wall, in the perennial bed and in the rock garden. I had no idea what they were. Then up popped these beautiful gaillardia. I was thrilled.

This year I saw a clump of leaves in the same place and thought to myself, I'll separate these and I'll have them all over the garden. It was a very large clump and as I meticulously divided it up I thought how lovely they would look, great splashes of colour. I checked them a lot; I watered them well and gave them manure tea; I stared and stared. Later on, a niggling doubt crept into my mind: Maybe it's not gaillardia that I've taken such good care of. I quickly squelched this thought. I felt like a traitor just for thinking it. I was always inspecting their leaves, turning them this way and that. Was this a small bud at last? Didn't they look a lot like forget-me-nots? No, they certainly did not.

The other day, I saw to my horror that one clump had definitely turned into forget-me-nots. How could they! Days later there were forget-me-nots all over the place. Where before I nurtured the pseudo-gaillardia, now I pulled out forget-me-nots by the ton. Ah well, the beauty of gardening is that there is always next year.

But strange, isn't it, how we delude ourselves? If I hadn't been so set on having gaillardia I might have spotted my mistake much sooner. It isn't the first time I've been

deluded; I've mollycoddled goldenrod, cherished mustard and once my zinnias turned into lettuce.

I had seeds of a plant called White Swan coneflower. I love purple coneflower and thought that a plant with "white" in its name would of course be white. I had visions of drifts of beautiful white coneflowers, a rarity, because I failed to find any mention of them in my garden books. I germinated the seeds and took care of them. That first year, I'm glad to say, I got leaves that looked like coneflower leaves. The next year they flowered. Bright purple coneflowers. I didn't believe it, of course, and kept waiting for them to turn white, which I was sure they would. I waited and waited. They did eventually turn white, when snow fell on their little seed heads.

So that's how come I have no gaillardia this year or White Swans either.

You'll be surprised to know I've been thinking about design. What I'd really like in this garden is to be able to walk out of the front door, turn right through the gap in the lilac hedge, and see down to the other end of the garden without the view being interrupted by piles of rotting wood propped against the garage plus an ancient black slate grate that came out of the house and weighs a ton. It would mean moving the wall back and I'd like to curve it. By doing this, instead of a narrowish walkway I'd have a decent width, for even more junk! No, no, no! At the end of this "vista" is a tub of nasturtiums that look sickly later on in the summer. I wonder about gaillardia there instead, with of course a couple of forget-me-nots. When all this has been accomplished, coming through the lilacs and looking at a tub of gaillardias will be like a burst of happiness!

Love, Judy

163

Water Lane
West Vancouver, B.C.
July 18

DEAR JUDY,

Can you believe this! Like you I started White Swan coneflowers from seed last year. I planted them at the top end of the pond in an area I'm planning to reserve for white flowers. When the buds formed a few weeks ago, I was convinced they were paler than the regular coneflowers planted just a little way away and, like you, I was still convinced when the petals began to open. It was only after your letter arrived that I could see, beyond a shadow of a doubt, that my white swans are purple ducklings — and I'm not pleased. White Swans *are* supposed to be white. Unfortunately I can't remember which company the seed came from. Can you?

It's true that disease-resistant varieties of elm have been developed. As far back as 1939 the Dutch introduced a variety of the smooth-leaved elm called Christine Buisman, and several others followed in the States, but they didn't have the size and fountain shape expected of an American elm, until the University of Wisconsin produced 'American Liberty'. We haven't heard much about this variety in Canada. I don't know why.

I like your idea of moving the wall back. It'll be quite an undertaking, but I'm sure you'll manage somehow.

A year ago, I began to plant the border beside the circular driveway and this seems a good time to review its progress. Here's my report:

On the credit side, much growth. Things really move fast

here. Even the ground cover of bearberry is reaching out like flat green octopus (octopi?) trying to touch tentacles. Roll on the day they link arms!

On the debit side, one invalid, one convalescent and one clear case for the shredder.

Ray's magnolia settled in well and even treated us to lovely, muted pink flowers. To dwell in the vast pool of shade cast by its six-metre spread of boughs-to-be, I chose shrubs that are usually described as shade loving. As often as not, this means shade tolerant. But loving or tolerant, the rhododendrons and viburnums will have to put up with sun for a while because our magnolia still stands a puny two metres and barely casts a shadow. Keeping the shrubs well watered hasn't been a problem so far this year and I've given them a mulch of my precious pine needles.

The shrubs we moved have done well, though the large camellia still looks a little pale and the lily of the valley bush was definitely a mistake. Its new growth was more brilliantly pinkish orange than I dreamed possible and didn't blend at all well with my subtle colour scheme. If you can imagine Tina Turner in concert with the Welsh male voice choir, you'll understand. Tina is back in the jungle waiting for a more suitable gig.

Two of the rhododendrons I bought fared badly. One of the Snow Ladies turned a blotchy yellow in May for no apparent reason. It certainly wasn't lack of water, not after a month of steady rain. A soil test gave a pH reading of 5.6, comfortably acid for rhododendrons, so it wasn't a problem with alkalinity either. Disease? Essential trace elements missing from the soil? I was considering a dose of epsom salts (five millilitres in a litre of water sprayed onto the foliage is apparently a quick fix for magnesium deficiency), when I noticed the tell-tale rainbows of a miniature oil slick running from the car's parking spot, across the asphalt driveway, right into my lady's lap. Poisoning! If she hadn't succumbed to oil she'd almost certainly have drowned. I quickly moved her to drier land where she's making a slow recovery. Meanwhile the car has been serviced and we've persuaded the driveway to drain into the storm sewer. More trenches of course.

When I came to plant *Rhododendron* 'Elizabeth', I discovered a solid mass of roots spiraling inside the plastic pot. It's almost impossible for a plant like that to develop normally and I usually pry the roots apart with my fingers. Elizabeth's, however, were more tightly girdled than the feet of a Mandarin princess and I resorted to surgery. I made several shallow slits from the sides at the top of the root ball, then I made one deeper cut up from the bottom and splayed the split halves apart. This is supposed to be the proper treatment for severely pot-bound plants; it's called butterflying. Sadly, Elizabeth's life as a butterfly was short. She flew straight to horticultural heaven.

My operation was probably hamhanded, but even in skilled hands, butterflying is a desperate measure. The real solution is simple. Don't buy pot-bound plants! Never again will I buy a pot that is light to handle even when the soil is damp, or a pot with roots pushing out of the drainage holes, or with a tell-tale ridge around the rim where circling roots have forced the earth up.

Rhododendron 'Surrey Heath' was a chance discovery at a garden centre. I bought it because I liked its compact looks and because I'd read somewhere that Surrey Heath is A

Good Thing. And it is, though I've noticed the weevils think so too. It has neat, pointed foliage and deep pink buds which open to a paler tone. To call it pale pink hopelessly misses the mark, for the petals seem to shine with an inner light. This spring, I sped back to the garden centre for a second helping, and here the Surrey Heath mystery began. Surrey Heath? They'd never had such a plant, never heard of it! Could they get one for me? Maybe next year from the States. I wasn't going to hold my breath. I've checked round all the local garden centres and drawn a blank. I can't even remember where I read about it in the first place.

There was a time when I thought that only a fool would plant things one year and dig them up the next. So whenever I needed to extract an apricot lily, say, from the over enthusiastic embrace of red bee balm, I was burdened with shame. I've even been tempted to sneak about under cover of darkness to make surreptitious rearrangements in a flower bed. Not any longer. Now part of my creed is *blessed are they that shuffle shrubs, for theirs is the joy of gardening*. I'm such an inveterate shuffler, I suspect my rhododendrons cringe when they see me coming. But at least I'm not the only indecisive gardener around. The owner of one fine English garden had the plants moved about so often, the exasperated gardener finally stormed, "Why don't you just leave the bleedin' things in the wheelbarrers!" An understandable outburst but my sympathies lie with the owner.

Gardens are a process, aren't they? When I draw planting plans for private gardens, I explain that this is only the kicking-off point. It's no use stepping back and watching the game from the sidelines. No matter how carefully I (or anyone else) design the spacing and combination of plants, the scheme will end up a shambles unless someone cares enough to referee.

Most gardeners probably catch on to this at a much earlier age than I did. I blame my tardiness on education. I was taught to get it right first time, which is all very noble and necessary if you're piloting a jumbo jet into Pearson International Airport or planning a contract landscape that has to look like a million dollars for a grand opening. If you're pottering round your own garden with a spade and a bunch of baby plants, the notion of once-and-for-all is a worse killjoy than clay.

If, as I move Surrey Heath(?) for the third or fourth time, I feel twinges of guilt, I'll remind myself that Alexander Pope, who was no fool, wrote almost three hundred years ago:

> *My trees and shrubs will indeed outlive me if they do not die of their travels from place to place, for my garden, like my life, seems to me every year to want correction and require alteration.*

July 19

The boarders arrived this morning. No! We're not going into the Bed and Breakfast business; it's the local term for dry-wall plasterers. We're going to do all the interior trim and finishing ourselves so we don't have an estimated date of completion but are planning to move back into the office regardless. Ray is beginning to bounce off the dining room walls.

The construction hasn't been without drama. A concrete cutter sliced through the water main with his electric saw and produced a spectacular fountain in the office until the fire brigade arrived in all its splendour to rescue us. Our builder was left hanging by one hand from the roof when the scaffolding gave way under him (at least he didn't damage my roses), and our boarder has just tripped and fallen off his stilts (we don't think his leg is broken).

I think we need a holiday.

With love, Elspeth

Hampton
July 23

At last I've started. Two weeks ago I began pulling down the old wall just outside the kitchen window. Ever see the movie The Wooden Horse? *About some prisoners in a camp in Germany during the war. They dug an escape tunnel and had to get rid of a lot of earth without the guards knowing. I feel just like 'um. I have all this excess earth to get rid of. I think they hid it in their pants. I don't have to do that. But I still don't know what to do with it.*

JAM

Kennebecasis River Road
Hampton, N.B.
July 27

DEAR ELSPETH,
For a long time I wondered if I had the staying power to move the wall back about a metre and rebuild it. I should have kept wondering because it looks like hell out there right now, with stones all over the place to say nothing of the piles of earth I don't know what to do about. My aim is to push the flower bed that runs along the top of the wall into the sunlight. With all the effort I'm expending, I could be pushing it into the next century.

My father and I built the original retaining wall when we first moved into this house. In places it's almost a metre high. The stones in it are not the flat ones that I like so much, but are all shapes and sizes, difficult to handle and difficult to place. Many of them are field stone that came from the old barn; some, which have a curved edge, came from an old well, and others I picked up at the side of the road. Flat stones are something I can never resist and am always dragging them home.

I would be a bit further along if it hadn't been for the incessant rain, every other day it seems. Since I've dug down to clay the water isn't draining away. It's a pond I should be digging. I've always wanted one. But at least the monsoons give my back a rest.

Another thing that has delayed my progress is a wasps' nest I disturbed. Fierce little orange and black wasps came buzzing angrily out of a hole in the wall. I ran, but couldn't get away from them; they chased me all over the garden. I

even hosed down their hole to try and get rid of them; perhaps that's why they are so damned mad. One or two are still hanging around the spot where their nest was, and as soon as they sense I'm there, they start after me again. Between the heat and humidity, wasps and mosquitoes, I feel I'm in a war zone. Pity I wasn't around when the Panama was built. And not to be forgotten are the snakes who lived in the wall. Shortly after I'd started my excavations I saw a pair of them slither out. Later, I found them curled up together on top of the compost.

As you know, this is not my first wall. Apart from helping my father on this one, I've built quite a number in my haphazard way. I love a good stone wall.

After I've pulled a few layers of large stones down it seems an avalanche of smaller ones spill out; they are everywhere and I don't know what to do with these either. I remember my father throwing shovelfuls of small stones in behind the large ones. Maybe he didn't know what to do with them either. I imagine him looking down at me now and just shaking his head. I try and move the bigger stones out of the way so that I'll have room to work and then I rake the rest of them into piles of small, medium and large stones, but the more I rake the more I get, rather like eating tripe — the more you chew the more your mouth fills up.

When I've moved a portion of the old wall I start digging the earth out. In some places I dig through hosta roots and pull out masses of vetch, monkshood and bee balm; the lovely smell from the bee balm perks me up no end. Then I separate the earth into a pile of good topsoil and several piles of not-so-good soil. These, along with mounds of stones, are lined up against the house and make it look as if I know what

I'm doing. Which of course I don't.

In complete bewilderment, I lean on my shovel, look at the muck, kick a couple of stones and wonder about myself! Oh, for a slave called Hildegard!

You are lucky, you only move plants.

Love, Judy

 Water Lane
West Vancouver, B.C.
August 4

DEAR JUDY,
Remember Surrey Heath, the rhododendron that went missing? Well, it's found. I've just come across it in a nursery specialising in rhodos (a nasty word but better than mums and glads). They must also have heard that Surrey Heath is A Good Thing because they're propagating it by tissue culture. So now I have three tiny clones, as well as my original, to move around the garden.

I could use some of your stones — small ones. I need them for the path around the pond. When we came, the path was surfaced with crushed limestone and weeds in about equal quantities. To remove the weeds, I have to dig everything up, and the limestone gets thoroughly churned into the soil — a great improvement. I've never liked the harsh grey of crushed limestone. Most of the weed is creeping speedwell and, when I started the weeding, it was in flower. It's an insidious little pest but its tiny flowers are such a heavenly and tender blue I felt like a ravaging brute when I ripped them out. It's easier now that the flowers are gone. Ray's trench accomplished some of the weeding for me but I still haven't finished the job.

I want the path to look completely relaxed and informal and my first thought was to pave it with flagstone laid on sand, like the sandstone "crazy paving" you laid to your front door. Sandstone and slate are available here — at a price — but the local rock is granite and although it makes fine walls it's not great laid as a walking surface.

The soil is gritty and full of pebbles and, as I was working my way through the speedwell, it dawned on me I could improve the soil and the path at the same time. So as I clear the old path, I've been laying out a roll of landscape fabric. Then as I dig, I pick out likely looking pebbles and chuck them into a large plastic pot. When it's full, I hose the stones clean, letting the mucky water drain back onto the beds, and dump the laundered stones onto the fabric. You can probably tell that I'm rather impressed by the efficiency of my system, and the price is definitely right. The stones are lovely colours, especially when they're wet, and look very much at home, which of course they are.

The trouble is, it's taking me forever. I don't know why. Maybe I really do need a holiday. It's also taking an unbelievable number of stones. I wonder if Anne would like to chuck a few my way. Which reminds me, I should explain to her why I've been prowling round the garden at night with a flashlight.

Besides the slow progress, there are other snags with the new path. One of our big cedars overhangs a corner of the pond area and constantly drops debris over everything. I don't mind raking the stuff off the beds but it's a pain to pick it off the pebbles, piece by piece. The rough surface also makes for slightly uncomfortable walking, though I tell myself this path isn't meant for speeding; it's for dawdling. Maybe the pebbles will slow me down enough to let me smell the lilacs.

As it happens, there is a lilac between the pond and the heap of rubble which, one day, will become the courtyard. The flowers are a lovely cream colour but the leaves are plagued by leaf miner. Lilacs do better in the east. My image of a typical New Brunswick house is of white painted gables with gingerbread trim, weathered shingle outbuildings and a clump of purple lilac. You see how nostalgia has already coloured my memory? The typical New Brunswick house is really a vinyl-sided split level with a pair of cedars out front. Sophie was once driving a foreign visitor round the province and was asked if the narrow trees flanking the front doors had special religious significance!

I'm fussy about the materials I use for paving. I've been wondering what to use for the walkway to the office door. A few weeks ago, I saw, in a landscape supplier's yard, heaps of old cobble stones (I should really call them sets because they're granite blocks, not rounded stones). I think they were quarried originally on Nelson Island, up the coast from here, and had been laid in the streets of Gastown, the oldest part of Vancouver. With a century of traffic, their upper surfaces had been worn smooth, and running my fingers over them I could almost see the horse-drawn carts and early settlers. I wanted them so badly I couldn't sleep at night for thinking about it. The cost was far more than I felt we could afford but, at the end of a restless week, I mentioned them casually to Ray. After another week I persuaded him to drop in to look at them, as we just happened to be on that side of town anyway. To my horror, most of them had just been shipped to the States. I was so upset I didn't care about the cost any longer and said I'd take every single cobble they had left.

They arrived a few days ago and I couldn't be more pleased if they were ingots of gold. They are stacked up behind the house; not as many as I'd like but enough to reach from the driveway to the office door with some left over for the courtyard too.

We arrived home from a site visit a few weeks ago, to find a mysterious present on the doorstep. No note, no explanation, just a blue plastic bucket with a lid made from foil punched with holes. We stared at it for some time before Ray gingerly peeled back the cover. "Water," he said. Quite an anticlimax. I was expecting at least a kitten, possibly snakes. But the gift was not just a bucket of water. It turned out to be a bucket of tadpoles. I was thrilled.

We tipped them into the pond, they disappeared in a flurry of mud and we haven't seen them since, but we're sure some will survive to start a new colony.

Our benefactor remained anonymous until I talked to Doreen on the phone recently. She had mentioned to her son-in-law how much I missed having frogs around. Sean, bless his heart, decided to bring us some tadpoles from the lake near their family cottage. They are probably western tree frogs but he thinks there may have been some toadpoles (?) in there as well. He used Doreen's kitchen sieve to catch them, which I thought showed courage as well as initiative. I called to thank him and I really meant it when I told him that he couldn't have given me a nicer gift, except perhaps cobble stones. He promptly produced a few of those as well. What a man!

I do hope you survive the wasps and the weather, because I'm looking forward to the next episode of The Wall.

Love, Elspeth

P.S. I've just heard on the radio that there's a scheme to reconstruct a portion of the Great Wall of China in Nova Scotia — can they be serious? — and I thought of you immediately. This could be the job you've been waiting for!

 Kennebecasis River Road
Hampton, N.B.
August 11

DEAR ELSPETH,
Maybe building the Great Wall of China is a job come true. I would learn how to do it properly, but I don't have a Mandarin to teach me Chinese. Rain and mud have stopped my construction activities and all day today I've been waiting for the tail end of a hurricane to strike!

This morning, in gently falling rain, I went out into the garden wearing two navy plastic raincoats, both torn; one is thigh-length, the other reaches to my calf. I wore rubber boots and a Tilley hat over a bedraggled scarf. Tom said I looked like a pioneer.

I wanted to stake stuff before the high winds got here. I started with the very tall white nicotiana in the front flower

177

bed, the one that seems more leaves than flowers (I think it's *Nicotiana sylvestris*). Then I tied up some cleome and tightened up the beanpoles, collected rakes, trowels and spades, and put them in the garden shed. I reeled up the hose and took pots of geraniums, godetia and something, whose name completely escapes me, into the shed. I made sure my beautiful new watering can with the brass rose, and my new riddle — both of which I got for my birthday — were safe. D'you ever say "riddle"? It's a funny word. I think most people say "sieve."

I enjoyed gathering up tools and tying up plants in gently falling rain. There is something infinitely soothing about fine rain. I didn't want to come in.

Next day:

Last night the wind started about midnight, wild from the east; it sounded like crushing glass. I prowled around the house about 4 a.m. and looked out through the window just as the power went. Outside the kitchen window, I saw the lone sunflower, grown from bird seed, whirling like a dervish. Back in bed there seemed to be a lull as though the storm was satisfied it had done what it set out to do. But the wind soon came back in full force and blew all night, fading gradually towards morning. I feel apprehensive about going out into the garden, afraid of what I'll see.

Later:

Well, yes. Things have been pushed around. A clematis that was just coming into blossom lost many of its flowers. I accidently broke off a stem when I was trying to tie it up. Naturally it was the stem with the most buds. This clematis has never done well here. I think I shall move it, if the wind doesn't move it for me. The nicotiana in the front bed was OK, but the ones at the back of the house have all had their heads blown off; they were next to the scarlet runners that are now lying on the ground in what is the most sheltered spot in the garden. That's a hurricane for you. A milk crate and a wooden box that I'd used to protect seedlings were neatly taken up by the wind and placed side by side at the bottom of the back steps.

The poppies still have their heads bowed and shoulders shrugged as though they are protecting their hairdos. Branches of trees and tiles from the roof litter the lawn. Some delphiniums have been broken off, dark and light blue. I gathered them up and cleaned off the battered blossoms, then added nicotiana and Michaelmas daisies and took them into the house. I was so pleased to have them inside I went back out again and picked a bunch of black-eyed-Susans and snapdragons.

By the way, why *do* you go out at night with a flashlight?

Love, Judy

 Water Lane
West Vancouver, B.C.
August 24

DEAR JUDY,
I was thinking about you as we followed the progress of the hurricane up the east coast. It was a relief to hear that you

and the garden survived without major damage.

Staking plants is all very well but there may be an easier way for you to deal with wind. I've been reading about the doctrine of sympathetic magic. It's a close cousin to the doctrine of signatures which is that old belief about plants indicating their medicinal use by their appearance.

According to the doctrine of sympathetic magic, the plant for you is the lentil. Why? Well, lentils produce flatulence, right? In other words, they're windy. So all you have to do to protect young plants from wind damage is to sow a hedge of lentils round them. Like setting a thief to catch a thief. Honestly, I didn't make this up. No doubt a small shelter belt of lentils really could help to break a breeze, but I wouldn't guarantee that cans of baked beans buried round the garden would give you complete immunity against the next hurricane so perhaps you shouldn't abandon the twine just yet.

We've been away. Ray had business in Victoria last week and we were both feeling so exhausted, we decided to snatch a four-day holiday on Vancouver Island. It's been years since we had a holiday and we couldn't get the hang of it at first. It took us a couple of days to unwind but, in the end, good food, a hot tub and a beautiful beach did the trick.

I like to explore a beach, not lie on it. My ideal shore has plenty of bird life and interesting tidal pools. This one was short on pools but had plenty of interesting seaweed instead, so interesting I couldn't bear to leave it all behind, and we spent our last afternoon stuffing free fertiliser into draw-string garbage bags and loading them into the trunk of the car. The luggage took a back seat. I've seen your face light up at the prospect of free blackberries or a bucket of gravel so I know you'll understand how smug we felt, driving home in glorious sunshine with our haul.

Rob and Kimi had been house-sitting and we'd offered them the car for the evening so, after supper, Rob went out to unload the precious cargo. A few moments later he reappeared with an odd look on his face.

"I think you should come out," he said. "Something's going on."

Holidays are tiring. I was ready to flop and I didn't care what was going on.

"There's a noise," he insisted.

"What kind of noise?"

"I've no idea."

"For goodness sake!"

Wearily I followed him to the door.

"Well?"

"Listen!"

I listened. Even at a distance I could hear it; the car was definitely hissing.

"Come closer!"

I stepped forward cautiously. Closer, it sounded as if we'd locked a hailstorm in the trunk. I stepped back.

"Aren't you going to look?" I said and stepped farther back. Rob unlocked the trunk, threw it open, and leapt aside as a million small missiles hurtled into the air. Sandhoppers ricocheted off the lid of the trunk. Sandhoppers swarmed and bounced among the bags. Sandhoppers spilled out onto the driveway.

We stood open-mouthed. I still can't believe ten garbage bags held so many living creatures.

"Time to catch the bus," said Rob, but with a little motherly persuasion he agreed to take the car as arranged, and, one by one, we unloaded the bags, grasping them at arm's length and shaking hoppers off our sleeves. We dumped them on the driveway where they quivered and crackled and leaked a steady stream of escapees. Then we turned our attention to the thick layer of shore life seething in the bottom of the trunk. My first thought was to shovel it up. Hopeless! Shovelling water would have been easier. The vacuum cleaner was the answer (I wonder if vacuum cleaners play such a large role in the lives of other gardeners?) but after

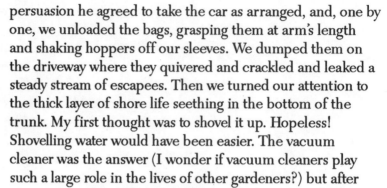

every visible hopper had rattled up the tube, the car was still buzzing angrily. The spare tire compartment! It was almost dark by the time we'd sucked up the last signs of life.

I dumped the bulging vacuum bags in the compost and I'm hoping fervently that sand hoppers need sand. If they take to egg shells and rotting potato skins we're in trouble.

The residue of all this, the seaweed itself, is now piled beside Ray's vegetable patch, though *piled* is an exaggeration. There must be easier ways to earn a few buckets of humus.

I've just reread your last letter and you ask why I was wandering round the garden at night with a flashlight. I hunt slugs. And weevils in season. I use a kitchen fork to flip the slugs into a yoghurt container, then I flush my catch. It isn't nice but it seems to be necessary.

I usually set a few beer traps as well, but slugs have an excellent sense of smell and I always feel I'm inviting every tipsy mollusc in the neighbourhood round to our place to party.

While we were away, I left a few traps untended and, when I finally came to empty them, the smell of the decomposing contents was so indescribably revolting, I think it may have put me off beer for life.

Love, Elspeth

 Kennebecasis River Road
Hampton, N.B.
September 13

DEAR ELSPETH,

Are you sure you still have seaweed? Check to see if the sandhoppers haven't carried it off. Sophie and I went down to Duck Pond on Sunday and seeing the seaweed on the beach she said, "We can take this home for the garden." I told her of your experience so we reluctantly left it there. She asked if I'd like to take some stones home. I said, "That's one thing I don't need. *Stones.*"

I've had to abandon the wall for a while because I can't get rid of the damned wasps. Their homing instinct must be very strong. So instead I thought I might paint an old rectangular sink that came out of our kitchen and is probably about a hundred years old. It is cast iron and enamelled, and of course heavy — what isn't? I dragged it into place under the flowering crab. I'll fill it with water and use it as a bird bath. I figured they'd enjoy a drink or a bath under the tree. Maybe this is why the neighbours have had their deck extended and a hot tub put in; they thought I might be getting ahead of them.

I enjoyed it out there in the sun, listening to the birds, singing away to myself, and painting the sink. It's an Oxford blue. I put on two layers and a layer of mosquitoes in between. Now it's not just a nice shape but a lovely colour and an interesting texture. After the paint dried I put a large flat stopper over the hole and watched the water seep slowly out. Then I applied a thick coat of Vaseline to the stopper and watched the water seep slowly out. After that I put on a thicker layer of Vaseline and this time it took all night before the sink ran dry. Now I've tipped the whole thing up so the water isn't over the hole at all. It's not so much the big hole that's the problem as the three smaller holes that took the bolts that held the strainer — that lived in the house that Jack built?

Over the stopper I put an orange plastic dish held down by a flat stone; I also put in large round pebbles for the birds to perch on, but so far no one has shown up — like having a party and nobody comes. While I was working on the wall, I left buckets of topsoil standing around and they became waterlogged from all the rain. Every evening, chickadees came to drink at the Bucket Hotel; why there and not at the Blue Sink Café? Sophie stopped in for a cup of tea; she saw the orange dish in the blue sink and asked, "Is that a goldfish in there?"

Bee balm grows along one side of it and I've put pots of

impatiens around the other. It would be nice to have blue flowers to match the blue of the sink; do I mean like matching shoes and purse? Something I've never managed. You gave me blue Siberian iris years ago, and they are beautiful, but I think I'll need a chain-saw to cut through the root stock.

Do you have any ideas?

Oh, your slug traps — how do you make them? Are they like mouse traps?

I was just looking through the window at the sunset. A mist has rolled in over the marsh and I can just see the ghostly silhouette of the trees; the hills are outlined in vermilion gradually merging to the palest pink.

Love, Judy

 Water Lane
West Vancouver, B.C.
September 23

DEAR JUDY,
There has been a peculiarly fishy smell in the car lately. It's especially strong when the weather is damp (which is most of the time). I'm afraid we didn't get all the sandhoppers out of the trunk after all.

You ask about slug traps. Mine are made from margarine tubs with two little doors cut into the rim. I sink them into the ground so the door sills are flush with the surface, and

185

when they're filled with beer I put the lids back on to keep the rain out. For the sake of appearances, I sometimes sprinkle soil on top of the lid.

At first I was using Guinness as bait, and it worked a treat but, after a few words with Ray, I visited the liquor store and asked for their cheapest brand. When I told them why I wanted it, everyone in the store got in on the act. Slugs, it seems, are as good as dogs and babies for breaking the ice round here. Anyway, the cheap stuff seems to suit the slugs just fine, even diluted with water, and it's also a great hit with the raccoons who pry the lids off my carefully prepared traps, lap up the contents, slugs and all, and fling the empties round the garden.

My cousin, Morag, has been over from Britain and on the first morning of her visit, we went for a walk with Anne. We'd hardly had a chance to admire the scenery when I noticed something like a ring lying on the ground. It was two slugs circling each other. Their manner seemed wary, like wrestlers weighing up the opposition. As we watched, the circle grew smaller until they were touching nose to tail. At this point we spotted a spike projecting from the right side of each head; strange location, but the intent soon became obvious. Can you imagine it — three middle-aged women in a huddle over two small slugs, entranced for half an hour? We felt like peeping Toms but couldn't drag ourselves away. My poor cousin! She must have had a strange first impression of life in Canada.

I can't get your blue sink out of my mind. I have some ideas for coordinated blue flowers; quite a few ideas. Remember, you asked for it!

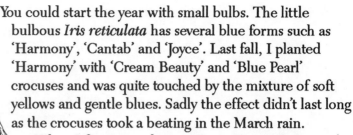

You could start the year with small bulbs. The little bulbous *Iris reticulata* has several blue forms such as 'Harmony', 'Cantab' and 'Joyce'. Last fall, I planted 'Harmony' with 'Cream Beauty' and 'Blue Pearl' crocuses and was quite touched by the mixture of soft yellows and gentle blues. Sadly the effect didn't last long as the crocuses took a beating in the March rain.

When I first grew these irises in Hampton, I wasn't impressed. They bloomed at the end of March and snow or freezing rain often took them by surprise. Here they start flowering as early as Valentine's Day, but if I see the slender stems toppled, I know to blame slugs, not snow storms. They are supposed to smell like violets, but I could never catch the slightest whiff of it until this year when I picked some and took them into the warmth of the house. The delicate scent fitted perfectly the classic elegance of the flower. Like snowdrops, they are so daintily wrought, so stylish and intricate, they reward any amount of close-up examination.

'Blue Pearl' crocuses aren't a pure blue and, to my mind, the irises have a touch of violet in them too, but there's no doubt about the blue of the squills. I've always loved the Siberian squill because of its true blue bells (you probably love it because it has Siberian in its name). Now I've discovered another squill which I like just as much. It's called *Scilla mischtschenkoana*, and was sold to me as *S. tubergeniana*, but please don't hold the names against it, because I'm sure it's your kind of plant anyway. I've seen it described as robust, and it is. I planted mine at the edge of the driveway and, just as they were coming through the ground, a truck ran over them. They kept right on coming and produced

Bulbous Netted Iris
Iris reticulata

their milky blue flowers as if nothing had happened.

Glory-of-the-snow, *Chionodoxa luciliae*, is a lovely sky blue. After it, comes the grape hyacinth, but beware of the form *Muscari comosum* 'Plumosum', the feather grape hyacinth. Instead of neat bells hugging the stem, it puts out wriggly distortions of nondescript colour. It's sometimes listed as 'Monstrosum' which sounds more appropriate to me as it's one of the few flowers I'd call ugly.

I know you're not short of forget-me-nots, but have you tried planting white narcissus among them? 'Blue Ball' forget-me-nots are a more vibrant colour than yours, and are supposed to be perennial. I grew them from seed at the farm and they stayed around for years but I think they were cheating and seeding themselves. Another vibrant blue is the lungwort, *Pulmonaria angustifolia*, a cousin to your William and Mary. I think I already told you about the kind called 'Mawson's Variety'. It looks wonderful as a ground cover among deciduous shrubs.

My favourite early perennial is the Virginia bluebell. It's a classy plant with flowers of discreet blue, like faded Wedgewood. I'm trying to establish some clumps of it here but the slugs like it as much as I do. The leaves die down quickly after flowering but you could plant a hosta nearby to cover the gap, or use annuals.

It's shady by your kitchen window, isn't it? The obvious blue annual for a shady spot is lobelia, which lasts much longer out of the sun. There's a cultivar called 'Cambridge Blue'. Do you think it would compete with the Oxford of your sink?

Do you know baby blue eyes? It's worth growing for the name alone and tolerates shade. Some pansies are called blue but they always look mauve to me, and so do *Ageratums*, but I wouldn't dare to suggest *Ageratums* anyway because I know you think they are miserable, fuzzy blobs and I agree. The bluest annual I ever grew was *Salvia patens*. It's really a perennial, though not in Canadian climates, and is slow to get going; you have to start it early to get your effort's worth. It prefers sun but is worth trying in light shade.

If you have borage in the garden it'll probably find its own way to the sink, it seeds itself around with such abandon. You don't get much flower for the quantity of leaf, but the blue is clear and you can crush the young leaves and add them to claret cup. So I believe. I sometimes wish I lived in the claret cup era. I could stand a little gracious Victorian living now and then, but on second thought, perhaps I'll settle for beer without borage and forego the claret with corsets.

For summer perennials, the cranesbill (true geranium) 'Buxton's Blue' is a possibility, though I'm doubtful if it's blue enough to hold its own beside your paint. The blue of other geraniums, like 'Johnson's Blue', varies in intensity with the season but there's always a touch of red in it.

I've seen plenty of articles written about blue flowers but the authors usually wander off into mauves and purples. I had a client who told me she wanted to plant blue rhododendrons. I felt I should point out that, in spite of names like 'Blue Bird' and 'Blue Diamond', the colour is really bluish mauve. She became quite agitated and promptly changed the subject. I didn't know what was wrong until her husband left the room and she explained that he detested anything mauve — was adamant about it — wouldn't have a mauve flower in the garden at any price. If, however, she called them blue he didn't seem to notice. I've hesitated to use the word mauve in front of a man ever since.

The most ethereal of all blue flowers is surely the delphinium. Most true blues don't mix well with lavenders, purples, turquoises and (pardon my language) mauves — they're usually better with whites and lemon yellow — but delphiniums manage to look great in a mixture. Maybe it's just that I think delphiniums look great, whatever. They're not, of course, shade-tolerant, acid-loving, slug-repelling plants, but I mean to grow them anyway and I know you do as well.

You can wake up now; I've finished.

Love, Elspeth

 Kennebecasis River Road
Hampton, N.B.
October 11

DEAR ELSPETH,
The wall is moving slowly — well, you know what I mean. I've moved so much earth, I'm beginning to feel like a bulldozer. Have also asked myself *why* I start these massive earth moving projects, even though this one is nearly finished. Had I not been hampered by mosquitoes, wasps, mud and incessant rain, it would have been done by now.

I spend a lot of time taking barrow-loads of wet earth to all parts of the garden. The truck that delivered last year's firewood drove over the grass and left deep ruts which I've filled with the stony sludge. Like a bloodhound, I search out depressions in the lawn and level them off. I've topped the ground around the beds at the front with prime quality earth and instantly — weed-free beds. Soon I'll be pushing the wheelbarrow down the street crying, "Soil for sale."

The best part is placing the stones. I try to put the huge ones at the bottom, and some of them are pretty huge. Squelching in mud, I manoeuvre them into place with a spade and a couple of crowbars. I'm probably doing myself irreparable damage because I don't move them once. I make a lot of mistakes — I move them again and again. It seemed much easier when I worked with my father; of course I was fifteen years younger and we both moved them into position and probably just once. Fitting the upper layers is light work after that, although I yearn for a load of nice flat stones.

I was raking the area in front of the wall when I came across a large flat stone half buried in the earth. I was tempted to leave it, but as you know I can't leave a stone unturned. I hauled it out and found that next to it were two more flat stones. So with crowbar and spade I dug them out, and made three steps in the wall. They don't look half bad either. I want to edge them with something. Lace? Creeping thyme? Phlox? It may not be sunny enough for thyme or phlox. I've already pressed hen-and-chicks into the crevices of the wall. I just couldn't wait!

It's still a terrible mess out there and I must try and rake up the small stones, get some good soil down and throw in some grass seed before winter sets in.

Later:
I don't know what date it is but you won't believe this. I was rushing out through the back door, eager to rake, and you

know the brick steps I made, well, I tripped on them and crashed into one of the garden chairs which collapsed and threw me back onto the steps. After all this falling about the doctor sent me to a neurologist who said my neurology was OK but that I'd broken my leg. A spiral fracture, so I have a cast from knee to toe — and I wasn't even running away from the wasps. About those wasps in the wall — I often thought of dynamite but that would get rid of the house as well — not such a bad idea. I shouldn't have said the wall was nearly finished.

I was sitting at the kitchen table gazing out at the wall, wondering when it would ever be done, when a large white dog, a Pyrenees I think, rushed past, dragging behind him a broken piece of red rope. He went to the blue sink and in one slurp emptied it.

The countryside of course looks very special at this time of the year. The colours take your breath away: oranges, burnished copper, burnt umber, ochre and a myriad of greens. Every year I say, "I think it's better than last year." But this year it really is. I also say that every year.

I was surprised and glad to hear you too use a kitchen fork in the garden. Once before I was surprised at something you did; you pulled out weeds and threw them behind taller plants. This astonished me because it was something I always did — because I'm slovenly. I don't know that I ever mentioned it to you but it made quite an impression. Strange, isn't it, how a little thing like that will stick with you? When my parents used to spend summers with us, my brother and his family often came to dinner. When the cry, "I haven't got a fork," went up, I dashed out and searched the garden for the forks I'd used to transplant seedlings.

I enjoyed your long list of blue flowers, even though I only needed about two names. I wonder if I'll be able to get any perennials in with this weight on my leg? Can you imagine the mauve-hating man and his blue wife as gardening buddies? He, in an absolute rage, tearing out anything showing the slightest tinge of mauve, without the slightest tinge of remorse. I'm not keen on mauve in certain plants either. It reminds me of an old aunt who wore a mauve crêpe dress. It was the colour of ageratum and was pinned at the neck with a brooch filled with plaited hair. She said the hair belonged to her fiance who *fell* at the Dardanelles. My mother said it looked more like the hair of a dog to her.

Odd you should mention the lungwort. I was given a clump in spring and was told it was the blue William and Mary, so I shall have to move it closer to the sink. You're right about borage seeding itself. It comes up all over the place. I read you can float the flowers in finger bowls. Well, yes... yes.

My best surprise bit of garden this year was from a packet of wildflower seeds. In spring when I was clearing out the gravel and stone path, I moved a stepping stone to get at the weeds and underneath found a foil packet of seeds that must have been there all winter. I had no idea what they were but sprinkled them on an empty piece of ground. Still blooming are red and blue flax, toadflax, poppies, some tall yellow daisies with small heads and a very pale version of the same, Siberian wallflower and many shades of cornflower. So far we've not had a killing frost. And talking of the gravel path, the alyssum that reseeds itself every year is just marvellous out there. Funny how plants seem to do so well in a medium they've chosen for themselves — like the gravel.

I've been practising walking and in spite of this new handicap, I've managed to plant my bulbs. It's a job that's been hanging over me for a while, because some years I have to use a pickaxe in the frozen ground. Last fall I planted pale pink tulips in the newly hatched bed around the four maple trees at the front of the house. In the spring, to my delight, pale pink forget-me-nots surrounded the pale tulips. I was amazed at how beautiful it looked. I can still see it; a delicate arrangement and all quite by accident though it looked as if I knew what I was about. This bed is so exposed I was concerned the wind would play havoc with the tulips but the wind seemed to go right over their heads. So I've bought more pink tulips and earlier on I planted more pink forget-me-nots.

There is never a shortage of forget-me-nots in my garden. They remind me of my grandfather's stone farmhouse in Wales; forget-me-nots lined the path going up to the front door and at the side of the house he kept cages of ferrets that he used for rabbiting. He died of drink.

I've not always been fond of tulips. I thought them very stiff and formal and was always tempted to salute them, but either they or I have changed. A few years ago I planted some practically black tulips, 'Queen of the Night', but over the years they have become smaller and smaller, not queenlike at all, more lady-in-waiting. I think the soil is poorly drained in that part of the garden and the damp has rotted the bulbs.

Last year I put in some Kaufmanniana tulips along the path leading to the house, thinking that because they are short they'd not have to battle the wind. I looked forward to seeing the path alight with "pure white blooms with a red rim aging to soft pink." I mean, you would, wouldn't you? They are supposed to be one of the earliest tulips to appear. But the "white rims aging to soft pink" never appeared — not one.

I wanted to dig some compost into the bed where the bulbs are to go, so I put a plastic bag over my cast and wheeled a load from the back of the house to the front... a few times it nearly ran away with me. While I was moving it, a couple walked by, pushing a stroller with a sleeping child. They were middle-aged and overweight and seemed to have used the same hair dye — they looked like a pair of leopards. Often when I work in the front of the house people stop and talk.

"Nice day, eh," said the male leopard. "Broke ya leg?" He continued in this strain.

"You shouldn't be on it like that, digging an' that. My sister broke her leg, didn't take care of it. Had to be broken again and reset. Walks with a bad limp to this very day."

Having spread comfort and joy the leopard family ambled

off. What's a limp anyway? I carried on regardless.

I hadn't realized how difficult it would be to dig in compost with a cast on. I pushed the spade in with my shoulders — sounds like I was standing on my head — using all my weight. It worked OK except that today my shoulders and upper arms are very stiff and sore and my leg aches and I don't fancy any more hard work which is why I'm indoors writing this long letter. (That sentence leaves me breathless.) But all that unusual exercise was great for the pecs and deltoids! After getting the compost in and kneeling as well as I could, I dug holes with the trowel and dropped in bone meal and bulbs. I noticed on the bags that *none* are the pale pink I had in my mind, but they *are* pastel shades such as Apricot Beauty and white Triumphator. I gave them my blessing and pushed the wheelbarrow back to the shed, limping all the way.

Love, Judy

 Water Lane
West Vancouver, B.C.
November 2

DEAR JUDY,
A broken leg! I'm so sorry. Good thing it's November or you'd be out there mowing the lawn as well as digging. I don't want to sound like a wet blanket, but don't you think the leopard couple may have had a point?

No frost here yet. October was pleasantly mild but I

missed the fall colours. Back east I thought of fall as a short sharp blast on the trumpets; defiance in the face of winter. Here it's more like a requiem for summer played *andante*. It starts in September and in December the predominant colour is still green.

But fall here has its compensations. I was walking in the forest the other day and came to a clearing among massive trees. The sunlight filtered in from high above and the whole space shimmered with the silvery gauze of cobwebs. It was as if the air itself had suddenly become visible. Breathtaking! In the forest, at this time of year, I've learned to wave a stick in front of me as I walk. The paths are criss-crossed with webs and, beautiful as they are, it's not much fun to walk face first into them.

Spiders here, like the trees and the slugs, are extra large. This house had been empty for some time when we first moved in and the basement spiders had taken over. Basement spiders seem to have been designed for Hallowe'en. They're big as mice, beetle black and fast as the devil. I lived in terror of them till Moses came to my rescue. He finds them tasty as well as amusing.

I'm squeamish about spiders inside the house but, strangely, not outside, so I didn't mind when a large garden spider took up residence outside our kitchen window early in the autumn. Because he had a missing leg, we called him Seven. He spun magnificent webs and the kitchen light attracted plenty of flying insects, so Seven grew fat. Eventually, however, the colder blustery weather took its toll and the web began to come apart at the seams. One morning, Ray announced that Seven was dead. Sure enough, the little crumpled corpse was hanging in a corner. I mourned over it as I washed the dishes. I kept meaning to go out and brush it away, but didn't of course, so there it stayed looking more shrivelled by the day, a melancholy reminder of the year's passing.

Then yesterday, a miracle.

A fly blundered into the remnants of the web. I thought its struggles were twitching the dead limbs, but no, Seven was alive. Slowly, he unscrambled his legs and started to move. Too slowly. The fly escaped. By this time I'd endowed Seven not only with a name, but with all kinds of human emotions: hope, perseverance, courage. I couldn't bear to add disappointment to the list, so I went out to the compost bin, trapped some fruit flies in a jar (I don't endow fruit flies with human characteristics), opened the kitchen window and shook them out. Success! One fly stuck and Seven grabbed it. Then, as I closed the window, I wrecked the entire web. Fool! It was typical, I thought, of clumsy, sentimental human interference.

But Nature forgave me. Today, the second miracle.

The web is restored and there, adding the finishing touches, is Seven himself, still scrawny, still fumbly, but back in business. This time I'll let good old Nature take her own course, though I may nudge her in the right direction by leaving the kitchen light on tonight to make sure breakfast will be served.

Evening:

The sun appeared so I went out to tidy around my Camperdown elm. It'll be the last cleanup of the year. I hope. It's been dropping debris all summer. This winter, I've decided to attack the scale and the aphid eggs with dormant oil spray. Have you ever used it? At the farm we sprayed it on our apple trees but it's a messy business and I had hoped to leave that kind of bother behind. The kind that's available in Canada is harmful to evergreens so I'll have to cover the groundcover of bearberry with plastic sheets. What a bother!

You know I'm no technological hot shot. It took me years to accept word processors, and microwaves are still beyond my cutting edge. So you can imagine my reaction to an advertisement I came across a few months ago, promoting trees and shrubs which install with an anchoring system involving small cement plugs.

The plants are made of plastic or, to be precise, alloy-reinforced, synthetic polyethylene-like compounds. According to the manufacturer, they are almost indestructible and yet look so lifelike, people have been walking past them for years without realising they were inert. *The plants,* that is. Believe it or not, two dozen varieties are available with optional snap-on flowers, buds and seasonal tints.

Ridiculous, right? But all my elm problems have made me think deeply about these everlasting trouble-free trees and shrubs. They come to mind whenever I am out there sweeping up, and whenever I remember all the shrubs I've had that grew too big, and Jill, the yellowwood tree who shrank until she wasn't there at all. To tell you the truth, there are times when the concept of horticultural perfection seems attractive. Think of it — no digging, no dirt, no disease, no death — the ideal solution for those who feel that gardening is eleven months of hard labour and one month of acute disappointment.

I've often wished plants would do what I expect them to. I've wished that mugo pines would stay at the height of a window sill, and that delphiniums would stand up without staking and flower from March to November. And plant breeders have tried to oblige. Look at the popular dwarf conifers. It isn't just their cuteness that appeals, it's their inertia. And marigolds. I expect a marigold to illuminate my garden at the specified wattage and, by golly, it does. I don't expect it to topple over in a breeze or suffer from sunstroke and, by golly, it doesn't. So now they're everywhere. Identical. MacMarigolds.

"Don't make a wish," somebody once told me, "it might come true." Well I did and apparently it has. The ultimate, perfectly predictable polyplant is now in our midst.

Gardens have always given us what we wanted most. I suppose if we'd lived in unhygienic medieval Europe, we'd have wanted plants to bathe us in cleansing aromas. If we'd lived in Persia, we'd probably have hankered after fresh fruit and the sounds of splashing water. What do we crave in our North American gardens? Good looks. Perhaps the notion comes from the lovely gardens we thumb through in coffee table books and magazines. It's that wind-and-weed-free, static and sterile, instant picture of loveliness we're after.

Is it?

Because if it is, then plastic is the logical answer.

But do we really garden just for appearances? Of course not. Gardens are for all the senses. But I think what matters even more to me (and to you) is the struggle itself, the very hands-on, knees-bent, mucky fingernail involvement we love to moan and groan about. We live in an age and a place that suffers from a surfeit of civilisation. Its trappings separate us from reality and what we want most from our gardens is the nose-to-nose encounter with the nitty-gritty, beastly and beautiful stuff of life. And death. We need to be part of it, know its tenacity and its fragility, feel its seasons in our bones. We need to curse it, adore it, sometimes to throw back our heads and howl in rage and wonder at it.

And, thank goodness, we don't need to snap on the seasons.

With love, Elspeth

Kennebecasis River Road
Hampton, N.B.
November 28

DEAR ELSPETH,
I feel just like Seven with an absent leg. And just like him, I've adapted. But it's to a cast and not to an amputation. I'm amazed I've become used to it so quickly. But I hope it will be off before Christmas and then I'll have to adapt all over again.

Yes, fall is a short sharp blast in defiance of winter, and right now the garden looks sad and dejected with only a smattering of snow. We need a good snowfall to cover everything up. The grass and shrubs look faded and tired; the clumped leaves of *Lychnis*, the tall one with magenta flowers, are a dull washed-out grey and the remains of the Maltese Cross are beige. Still I wouldn't change them for plastic plants. There would be no joy in them — their constant perfection, no flaws and no surprises, no turning a leaf to see if it's gaillardia or forget-me-not, no thrill at seeing

201

aphids *haven't* eaten every leaf, and no pleasure in watching them grow, or do they have some sort of electronic gadget that makes them appear to grow? I've seen live plants imitating artificial ones and have even snipped leaves off to see if they are real or plastic. Even then, I wasn't completely convinced.

I once had a nasty experience with artificial flowers. Not long after I was married, we worked our way around the States. One summer I worked as a waitress on Cape Cod. The restaurant was established in an old captain's house that was surrounded by enormous maples and oaks. It was very elegant. The china was antique and the napkins and tablecloths were linen; the expensive menu was in French, which only the chef understood. In the centre of some of the tables were artificial flower arrangements and we were told to remove them whenever we served fondue. Well, I forgot. I was serving a group celebrating a fiftieth wedding anniversary and the first thing I noticed was a strange smell. Then there were flames shooting out, chairs pushed over, and I was flinging glasses of water around like an underpaid fireman. The celebrant, a seventy-five-year-old man, thumped his chest and said, "Oh, I nearly took a heart attack," and I thought to myself, "Yeah, my days are numbered too."

Yesterday I managed to turn the blue sink upside-down for the winter. Its days too, might be numbered if birds don't drink or bathe in it. I think the sides are too deep and they can't see if predators are close by. I saw a chipping sparrow in there and it kept craning its neck to see over the top. But today a squirrel slipped down through the hole and came out underneath; then he and his companion ran around the

garden and zipped down the hole again. I sprinkled sunflower seed on the top of the upturned sink and flocks of grosbeaks have deigned to eat there. Their colouring is so exotic they seem more suited to the west coast than here. I'm happy that somebody likes my sink.

I've been trying to get Christmas cards off to Britain and was thinking about presents. I love getting gift certificates for nurseries; I can dream for months on end about what I shall buy. Though what I'd really like is a stump eradicator. What heaven to wake on Christmas morning and find all the old elm stumps on the front lawn have vanished! Actually they probably will have vanished — they'll be covered with snow. But I think nothing short of dynamite will shift them. I've heard of drilling holes in stumps and pouring in gasoline and setting it alight; I'd have the whole place in flames in no time at all, just like the restaurant. I'm no good with fire. When I used to burn stuff in the ditch, I'd spend ages lighting it and as soon as it was burning, I'd get cold feet and water it down with the hose. Then I'd spend the rest of the day trying to light it again.

The stump at the end of the driveway is massive. It has heaved up out of the ground and the roots are infested with

ants. A neighbour suggested I scoop out the middle and plant flowers in it. I'd be out there watering them all summer. I've managed to disguise one of them by planting a flower bed around it; the stump is all but covered with a Dropmore honeysuckle and surrounded by bee balm. Another stump is hidden by long grass and another is sprouting new elms.

I hate to be stumped by the stumps; if only Santa Claus came on a back hoe — a big one.

Love, Judy

 Water Lane
West Vancouver, B.C.
December 7

DEAR JUDY,
I wish I could give you a magic stump remover for Christmas but I'm afraid you'll have to settle for this picture instead. It shows the kind of stump that's common around here and it may make your elms pale into insignificance. To tell you the truth I'd love a stump like this, which is just more proof that gardeners are hopelessly perverse and covetous.

As you can see, these are no ordinary little protrusions. They are massive piles of timber that rise from the forest floor — and sometimes from suburban gardens — like crumbling castles. In the past, some of them really were hollowed out, roofed and used as dwellings. The early stumps still bear on their flanks the notches cut by loggers to

support their scaffold boards and I particularly like the way they carry, on their rotting crowns, the saplings of a new generation. Unfortunately we didn't inherit such a stump, nor do we have a nurse log, which would have been my second choice. Nurse logs are fallen trees that have decomposed enough for seedlings to root in them. Eventually the logs rot away altogether and their foster children are often left perched up on bow-legged roots like jockeys whose horses have bolted from under them. Hemlocks seem to root especially well in nurse logs and when you see large specimens growing in a straight row you know they were helped along in their childhood by a nurse who may have died a thousand years ago.

English garden designers of the eighteenth century liked to include ruins in their picturesque landscapes. The aim was to evoke thoughts of antiquity and lend that extra dimension of time to a garden. The landowner who wasn't lucky enough to find a ruin already lying about his property often felt obliged to build one, but when it came to creating a look of authentic delapidation, some people also had more luck than others. I've always enjoyed this extract from a letter by William Cowper, which I found in Joseph Wood Krutch's *The Gardener's World*:

> ... I went to see it: a fine piece of ruins, built by the late Lord Holland, at great expense, which, the day after I saw it, tumbled down for nothing. Perhaps, therefore it is still a ruin; and if it is, I would advise you by all means to visit it, as it must have been much improved by this fortunate incident. It is hardly possible to put stones together with that air

*of wild and magnificent disorder which they are
sure to acquire by falling down of their own
accord.*

I was also tickled to read recently that the ruined abbey at
Painshill Park in Surrey has now been restored — to a more
convincingly ruinous state I suppose, and no doubt at great
expense too.

When Ray and I visited Scotney castle in Kent, a few years
ago, the gardeners were pruning climbing roses which had
been trained over the picturesque ruins there. A young
fellow, obviously tired of fiddling with a plant that had
twined its way through an empty window, gave the stem a
sharp yank and dislodged not only the rose but the wooden
lintel and a good chunk of the wall above. We looked on in
horror as the heavy timber and an avalanche of stones
crashed into the rose bed. With a quick glance to make sure
his foreman was well out of the way, he grinned at us
nervously and explained, in a rich cockney accent, "Well see,
it's spowsed to be a ruin."

It wasn't only ruined buildings that were popular in the
eighteenth century. Did you know that there was also a
minor mania for planting dead trees? What would the
owners of those romantic and picturesque gardens have
given for a genuine dead cedar stump, a ready-made ruin,
with all its disturbing pathos and grandeur? There's antiquity
evoked! And in the case of the nurses, there's hope for the
future wonderfully symbolised into the bargain.

So maybe your old elms aren't so bad after all. If you
looked at them through romantic eyes, do you think you
could learn to appreciate them? In time you might even want

to restore them. No? Well, how about a real stump eradicator? They do exist, you know. Imagine! At great expense, you could have your problems ground to powder.

Talking about stumps, how is your leg? I do hope the cast will be off by the time you get this letter.

Seven, by the way, has vanished. I'm afraid nature took her course in spite of me. I've noticed that the Steller's jays have learned to flutter/jump up from the ground and snatch spiders from the wall of the house.

I've finally cleaned out the old petunias from the window box outside the kitchen window. I didn't do it sooner because there were still a few flowers on them. I've replanted the box with primulas and pansies and I'm hoping these will keep going well into the spring. They stand a good chance because the eaves are wide enough to keep off the winter rain. Their enemy here is not so much the cold as the damp.

I didn't know you'd been a waitress on Cape Cod. But maybe the job didn't last long?

With love, Elspeth

 Kennebecasis River Road
Hampton, N.B.
December 15

DEAR ELSPETH,
My cast has gone. When I first got it off I said, "That's not my leg." It looked brown and wizened. The technician told me to put a few drops of baby oil in the bath water to help

get rid of the dry skin. I did this, and the bath tub was so greasy I nearly slipped and broke the other leg.

I loved the William Cowper quote (especially "tumbled down for nothing"), but I can't get romantic about stumps, however large. I know most gardeners will make use of anything and will garden anywhere. The last time I was in England I visited a garden at a railway crossing. I spoke to the owner, a woman in her late fifties, who said she'd gardened there for thirty-four years and had six thousand plants. It was a small plot of land, but she had expanded her territory until it reached just over a kilometre along both sides of the railway line. I can imagine how thrilled she was when she dug the first plant in on the embankment and

realized she had thousands of kilometres of track to work on! How liberated she must have felt. The flowers at the side of the railway line looked like a water-colour, mounds of different shades, and clematis and honeysuckle climbing up into the trees. She gets up at four — just as it's getting light, and before the electric trains start — to work on the stretches alongside the railway. When I was there the trains whipped by at an alarming speed; it's a wonder she hasn't been killed as there's no space between the train and the embankment.

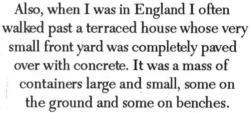

Also, when I was in England I often walked past a terraced house whose very small front yard was completely paved over with concrete. It was a mass of containers large and small, some on the ground and some on benches.

Each container spilled over with flowers. It was a wonderful display, proving again that you can garden anywhere.

I've decorated a large rose bush outside the back door with coloured lights. Actually, they were coloured a long time ago but are now quite clear. Over the years the rain has washed the paint off — I prefer them like this. In the strong winds, the rose bush adorned with lights looks as though it is waltzing. Some houses remind me of Caesar's Palace in Nevada, they are so heavily encrusted with Christmas lights.

Both boys will be home this year. As you know, I've never been in love with cooking but I found a booklet called *Cookies & Squares*, and have made such delights as Rum Balls, Heavenly Mocha Truffles, Chocolate-Apricot Pecan Balls and Nanaimo Bars. Now don't you wish you were here?

We've been having a really cold spell, with bitter winds but hardly any snow and right now I'm waiting for the washer to defrost yet again and the car engine to warm before I can get to the post office. Last night, going to bed, I looked through the window onto the marsh. Hanging in a velvet sky, above a cleft in the hills, was a pale lemon sliver of moon. The reflection in the silver ice on the marsh took my breath away. I remember a quote from Tennyson that describes this so well: "The long glories of the winter moon."

I hope you will all be getting together this Christmas. Will it be an eaves trough celebration this year? You have done well in getting your family to move to Vancouver; now if only your friends…

Have a good Christmas.

Love, Judy

Water Lane
West Vancouver, B.C.
December 17

DEAR JUDY,
I was in Chinatown yesterday, doing some last-minute
Christmas shopping, and took the chance to visit the Dr. Sun
Yat-Sen garden, which was built by Chinese craftsmen as a
replica of a Ming dynasty garden. I've been there several
times but always in the summer and I was curious to see it at
another season. Beautiful!

I've been thinking ever since about the design of gardens
in winter. In New Brunswick, gardens are a write-off from
the end of November to the end of March, and I used to hate
those English books that urged us to consider winter effects.
The effects I remember most vividly in the Maritimes were
those created by snow ploughs. Here, gardens really do exist
in winter, or at least they can, if the design is right.

Not only is the Chinese garden lovely at this time of year,
but the designers have managed, in an almost magical way, to
make a small plot of land seem endlessly extensive.

Eastern artists have always avoided clutter, have always
believed that *less is more*. Think of Japanese raked gravel
gardens. When Kimi's father was here for the wedding I
couldn't help wondering what he thought of our jam-packed
plot. I'm sure it must have seemed to him like a hideously
overcrowded party with everyone elbowing and clamouring.
My predecessors definitely subscribed to the Western
philosophy that *most is merriest*.

The Dr. Sun Yat-Sen garden is calm but never boring. As
you stroll through the interlocking pavilions, corridors and

courts, there are always glimpses of garden spaces beyond and sometimes there are stolen views of the outer world as well. It's as if there's a quiet voice following you round, saying over your shoulder, "Ah, but there's more."

And there is.

Each area, and even each plant or stone or building component, is loaded with meaning. A pine, for instance, symbolises strength, a bamboo, grace, and a flowering plum, the renewal of life. They're known as the Three Friends of Winter and certainly played their part when I was there, though it'll be some time before the plum flowers. Because of the symbolism, the sense of exploring an endlessly expandable space can be mental as well as physical and, to point your thoughts in appropriate directions, gardens of this type even have signs such as STUDY SUITABLE FOR FOUR SEASONS or PLACE TO CONTEMPLATE THE MOON.

I could use some signs in my garden but they'd be more like THIS WAY OUT!

Visitors to our kind of gardens might comment on the general atmosphere or the interesting collection of plants, but if they were to ask, "What does it mean?" they'd probably get a funny look, right? And yet meaningless gardens are a modern occurrence. You could almost say a modern aberration.

The meaningless garden began with the middle class. We're a pragmatic lot. If we make a formal garden, the central feature is more likely to be a bird bath or a barbecue than a symbol of monarchy and social order. If we put in a water feature, chances are it won't have much to do with God or creation, and our garden buildings are more likely to contain a lawnmower than a hermit with a philosophical bent.

As you can probably guess by now, all this pondering over the meaning of gardens has led me to ask myself, What does my garden mean? (I've already given myself a funny look, so you needn't bother.) The answer seems to be *a hell of a lot of work infusing order into chaos*.

I've been remembering Kathy's visit last year when I was so overwhelmed I didn't know where to start. It was when she put pick to earth that this garden really began for me and I'd like to have a symbol of "beginning" there. A sort of energy source. The spot is near the head of the pond so it could be a small bubble fountain or a trickle of water appearing mysteriously like a spring. Or it could be a piece of sculpture. I imagine a figure of a woman, not entirely an innocent but, like Thursday's child, with far to go.

A long way down the road I'll need another figure. It'll be at the foot of the garden, at the farthest reaches of the jungle, and there ought to be a bench there to rest (collapse?) on. Although it'll mark the final frontier, the figure won't be some kind of conquering hero. Creative endeavours, in my experience, don't culminate in any grand feeling of triumph. I'm not sure what this figure will look like but I know it'll be dark and almost obscured by greenery. At first I thought it might be the mischievous god Pan, but now it's taking shape in my head as a raven. Yes, definitely a raven. It's standing on the back of the bench and chuckling, "Ah, but there's more." And isn't that the truth!

Kate comes tomorrow. I can hardly wait.

Ray joins me in wishing you all a very merry Christmas (though it'll probably be New Year before you get this letter).

Elspeth

215

Kennebecasis River Road
Hampton, N.B.
January 3

DEAR ELSPETH,
You won't believe the snow and wind and the low, low
temperatures. You don't know what you're missing. But we
had a lovely Christmas, with both boys home and
complaining of the cold, of course. Our elderly neighbours,
who impress me more and more each year, came for
Christmas dinner and the elm stumps have completely
disappeared.

I was just outside filling the bird feeder that stands near
the crab apple tree. Where the grosbeaks had been slinging
around the tiny apples in their feeding frenzy, the snow was a
pale pink from the discarded fruit. It's as though someone
had gone over it with a pink wash. While outside I threw out
a handful of cranberries left over from Christmas... they
rolled around until they spelled HAPPY NEW YEAR! Then the
grosbeaks, chickadees and gold finches raised their little
beaks and sang out in chorus, HAPPY NEW YEAR! HAPPY NEW
YEAR!

Then I remembered you had been planting pansies and
primulas. How can you tell me this? All we have is an
abundance of flowering snowflakes — large drifts in certain
parts of the garden, and no two alike. They flower most of
the winter and some years well into summer. They don't do
well when brought indoors, which reminds me — I must
send you the honeysuckle cutting I potted up last year. It's
from the bush that originally came from you.

I don't think you ever saw my flowering crab. I must have

bought it after you left. I look at it often because it's just outside the kitchen window and you know how often we sat at the kitchen table. The young tree fell out of the trunk of the car when I was bringing it home from Brunswick Nurseries. I never felt that did it much good; it went into a slump, lost all its leaves, looked really sick, and I was in two minds whether to yank it out or not. I fed it weak manure tea, and suddenly, towards the fall, it started putting out small green leaves and has never looked back. Of all the trees I've planted this one seems to be in the right place for a change. It looks so contented with the pink snow drawn up around the trunk and the birds perched in the branches eyeing the feeder. I had suet pushed into the fork but it's vanished, and now the downy woodpecker goes up and down the trunk, turning its head from side to side looking for suet.

I never think a tree is a tree until birds have nested in it. The flowering crab may be too near the house and might never be bushy enough, but the lindens I got from you have all had nests, and I noticed, when the leaves fell from a young maple out front, it too had a nest. After the last snowfall, it had a cap of snow like an ice cream cone. Yesterday I saw footprints in the snow around the tree and the nest gone. I was happy to think someone wanted a nest badly enough to take it. Generally it's the car in the driveway they go for.

10:30 p.m.

Outside it is cold and dark and a storm is raging. We even have whitecap waves in the toilet. I'm warm and cozy in bed with flannel sheets and the new electric blanket David gave us for Christmas. It's wonderful. I've just finished a cup of hot chocolate, and was thinking how pleasant life is, lying here, safe and warm and having a good read.

In the magazine I was reading I saw an ad for a menopausal product... we could certainly both use it! It's a three-page spread; on one page is a photo of a woman gardening, on the second page it tells you about the product, and overleaf is a list of warnings.

It's the woman gardening who caught my eye. You should see her, co-ordinated all to hell! She's middle-aged with beautiful white hair and a face I'd love to have. And she's all in white! Imagine gardening in white. White turtle-neck, white shirt, white gloves, white pants and white shoes and socks; what's more, she's kneeling on a folded white pad. To make her look authentic, smudges of earth are smeared on her pants. She's holding a new cultivator, and the flowers she's working with are also white — chrysanthemums that look artificial. Coincidentally, I go to bed with Wilkie Collins every night. I'm reading *The Woman in White*, a melodrama I'm enjoying immensely.

Staring at the magazine woman in white made me think about how I look in my full gardening plumage. A freak. Co-ordinated, oh yes, in clothes left over from the boys, Jonathan's old shirts and sweaters and pants he's long grown out of and David's basketball socks and old basketball shoes and any old cap I can pick up. David said had I not had children I wouldn't have any clothes at all. I accidently caught sight of myself in a mirror once and said, "Is that you, Judy?" The other day, I came across my gardening pants thrown into the back of the closet; they were covered with earth, pockets full of string and unidentifiable seeds. I tossed them into the washer and they came out looking a lot better, but not white. I once saw a woman working in her garden, wearing on one foot a rubber boot and on the other a sneaker, and I know I would have liked her.

I've seen women in real life working in their gardens and wearing matching pink halters, shorts, shoes and visors. They are not real gardeners but arrangers. They don't relish getting their hands into the earth or become ecstatic over a plant that has survived the winter; all they seem to do is fiddle around with small patches of white gravel, the sort of gravel you've seen on graves in England.

I was reading a book about Vita Sackville-West, and in it was a photograph of her in gardening apparel. She was wearing men's breeches and high top lace-up boots and a good-looking shirt — somehow I don't think she was wearing her son's old clothes. I can't see her in basketball shoes or a baseball cap, but I do have a beautiful Panama for summer, and I can certainly see her in that.

As I'm getting off to sleep I shall be thinking of next season's gardening fashions. Maybe I should revamp my wardrobe: baggy pants with foam in the knees for easy kneeling and string tied just below the knee for warmth, a vest of many pockets, and an apron — the sort builders wear — with divisions for such as trowel and fork. A golf bag might come in handy for carrying the long-handled tools. I wonder if I'll dream of the woman in white.

Goodnight

Water Lane
West Vancouver, B.C.
January 11

DEAR JUDY,
So you wear your son's cast-offs for gardening. That's
interesting because so do I. And I do mean *your* son's. My
favourite gardening sweater is a cotton turtle-neck that once
belonged to David. He grew, and it was handed down to you.
Then it shrank and was handed further down — to me. So
there are advantages to being small, even if it's tough lugging
wheelbarrows. Do you remember the colour of the sweater?
It was white, but don't worry — I'm in no danger of turning
beautifully albino. I have no white gravel, no white
chrysanthemums, my hair is still red and the sweater has
weathered to a pleasant shade of beige, especially around the
cuffs. As it doubles as my favourite painting sweater it has
also acquired a sort of Jackson Pollock patina — quite
colourful, especially as I've just painted the bathroom yellow
and blue. It looks wonderful (the bathroom not the sweater)
and I'm longing to put a big jug of daffodils in there.

At this time of year, when it's dark and overcast for weeks
on end, I find myself craving yellow. Yellow and white.
Doreen tells me this signifies emotional disturbance. I think
it signifies lousy weather. I planted only white and yellow
bulbs in the window box along with the white and yellow
primulas and winter pansies, and then to top it off I stuck in
sprigs of golden variegated holly and ivy. How's that for
matching shoes and purse!

The unexpected arrival of winter for a couple of weeks this
year took the primulas and pansies by surprise and Moses

hasn't helped. He found that, sitting on the box, he could watch the wildlife in the garden while also keeping tabs on his food bowl in the kitchen. Although he has flattened the pansies he has hatched a couple of bulbs so all is not lost.

I'm sorry! I used to hate it when British Columbians boasted about their early flowers and now I'm at it again. Will you ever forgive me if I tell you that the daffodils are up? When the last snowfall cleared, there they were, under the elm tree. Of course they won't do anything dramatic for a month or two but in the meantime there will be the snowdrops and the winter aconites to keep my emotional disturbances from getting out of hand.

When nature came up with snowdrops and aconites, she must have thought gardeners were due for a break. Not only do they bloom at the same time, when we need them most, but they enjoy the same, cool damp conditions and look wonderful together. They are even propagated the same way, though I smile when I read that the best way to start a planting is not from bulbs in the fall but "in the green" from clumps moved after flowering. I keep hoping to meet a gardener willing to part with shovelfuls of aconites and snowdrops, but no luck yet...

This morning I noticed that Anne has a few snowdrops in flower. Of course I rushed — no, not for a shovel — to see if mine were out too. After poking about in the cedar debris I discovered a few promising green spears so at least a few of the bulbs I planted "in the brown" have survived. No flowers yet, though, and no aconites either. I'm planning to plant a few every year, hoping that, twenty years from now, there'll be enough to call a carpet. There's a picture in *The New Englishwoman's Garden* of the kind of thing I mean. It shows the trunk of a venerable tree and a grassy slope pale with snowdrops as far as the eye can see. Just as you'd expect, the scene is lit by watery English sunlight. The mood is demure and slightly melancholy so it comes as a bit of a shock to read the caption: *Snowdrops rioting in the moat*.

I don't think my ten snow-drop bulbs will give me much trouble. Indeed they won't have a chance because I'll pick them as soon as the buds fatten. It's easier to appreciate their perfect form and their fragrance when your nose is at tabletop level. Once, when I was staring absent-mindedly at a tiny bouquet, a bud sprang open in front of my eyes. It made a sound like a very small kiss, which made me feel absurdly privileged.

Do you have winter aconites? They're too squat for picking. The buds have no stem worth speaking of and look like yellow marbles lying on the ground. The stems keep growing as the flowers open and manage to raise the petals above the mud but you'd never call the finished product statuesque. So I think of them as the comics of the spring scene — cheery little clowns with ruffs and shining faces.

My poor Camperdown is in trouble again. I was stunned to notice, a week ago, that a gaping crack has opened from top to bottom of the trunk. I wonder if this is it then — the tremendous gas pressure Michael Dirr threatened? Have I found my horticultural true love only to have it explode?

But in spite of exploding trees and gloomy skies, I'm in high spirits. The reason? I'm planning a trip back east. Just me. I don't think Ray will be able to get away this spring.

Love, Elspeth

Kennebecasis River Road
Hampton, N.B.
January 19

DEAR ELSPETH,
Can you believe this? I've spent the better part of the day
working in the garden. WORKING IN THE GARDEN! I can
hardly believe it myself. No, I haven't moved, I'm still in New
Brunswick, though it's so mild I could well have been in
Vancouver. The ground, of course, is like iron and there are
no pansies and daffodils, but the snow and wind have gone
and a gentle mist softens the countryside. A reprieve from
the bitter cold. And I've been spreading mulch. I bet you'd
like to know where I got the mulch? What a trial that was!
   Anyway, the smell was marvellous, earthy and fresh like
spring; I felt the day was a gift to be used and spent well.
   Even the colours were a surprise: the grass was green,
seed pods the colour of chocolate, some jade-green rock
cress hanging over a wall and the dark red hen-and-chicks
filled the crevices like sealing-wax. The toba hawthorn —
such a beauty in spring — still had berries and between the
berries hung silver drops of rain.
   And I have spent the day well. I spread eighteen bags of
mulch along a fence in my ongoing war with the ground ivy
that comes and takes over the vegetable garden. It reminds
me of kudzu — the kudzu of the north. I've not seen it
enveloping telegraph poles and houses, but it does creep,
with great persistence, under fences. Though I will say, its
small blue flower has a lot going for it. But if it could just
keep itself under control!
   I put thick mats of old wet newspapers along the fence and

tried not to read about the Queen, the President or bloodshed in any part of the world. Then I heaved bags of mulch over the newspapers. I got so warm I had to take my coat and gloves off; my hands smelled wonderfully of pine.

It was very quiet out there because there were no birds around. The day before, the feeder was raucous with evening grosbeaks and three mourning doves settled on the ground beneath it. But today, not a single bird. I wonder if it's because of the sudden rise in temperature.

As I worked my way along the fence, I found myself humming a few leftover Christmas carols. I mulched around a clump of rudbeckia that I'd meant to move in fall, but didn't, then around a honeysuckle bush. Next to it is an ideal spot to put a clematis, a yellow one, *C. tangutica* is the one I'd like. The purple clematis that grew against the garage wall — it never seemed happy there — was torn out of the ground by the wind, so I have an excuse for a replacement. Even though I've placed the mulch thickly along the base of the fence, I'm sure if I looked closely, I would see the ground ivy gathering forces. Nothing will quell it.

It seemed a good idea putting the mulch down there and having a little path at the back of the vegetable patch. It will also make tending the scarlet runners much easier. I don't know why I haven't thought of it before. Often, in winter, I think of ways of making things easier in the garden, but in spring, when it's time to carry them out, they've vanished from my mind like snow. I'm really pleased with what I've done today. If only I could plant a clematis right away.

When I'd finished my activities I strolled around and admired my work. The mist hung softly in the air giving a gauzy surreal quality to the day. And the smell of evergreens was pungent. You can see I was quite euphoric. What a great start to a new year!

And to add to that, you think you may be coming this way in the spring. Will you stay with Kate, and then on to us? I imagine we'll never stop talking. I shall also want your advice on the garden. We could re-design the whole place!

Love, Judy

P.S. You mentioned snowdrops rioting. I read about a man who'd returned to see the garden he'd deeded to a national organization; he looked at it and said, "It's a floral haemorrhage."

 Water Lane
West Vancouver, B.C.
February 3

DEAR JUDY,
Of course I want to know about the eighteen bags of mulch. I'll bet they were free!

My trip is definitely on. I'm thinking of sometime in May, and will stay with Kate for a week or so. Could you have me in June?

The rain let up a couple of days ago and I went out to see how my bulbs were progressing. Horrors! The squirrels have made crocus salad of my lovely Blue Pearls. There's been a black squirrel here since we came and he sometimes dislodged the odd bulb but never indulged in theft and vandalism on a scale like this, not since the great walnut robbery. The trouble is he's been keeping bad company. A glamorous grey stranger is hanging round the neighbourhood with, I suspect, more than crocuses in mind. I predict a dynasty of bulb-chomping vermin.

You'd think that Moses would keep the wretched creatures at bay but he gave up chasing squirrels long ago. Still, he may have his uses. He's on dawn to dusk curfew because coyotes and even cougars have been seen in the area lately. They come down from the mountains in winter and have learned to prey on household pets. There are lurid reports in the papers along the lines of, *"All that was left of poor Curly was his collar," said a tearful North Shore poodle owner*. The result of the curfew is a supply of moist cat litter which I'm going to sprinkle sparingly round the crocus shoots as they appear. I'm not terribly optimistic about the results. These are bolder than average squirrels, cousins of the Stanley Park variety which climb the trouser legs of tourists to snatch sandwiches. Ah well, if a whiff of *Eau de Chat* doesn't do the trick, and if the cougars don't get Moses, maybe they'll get Blackie and Gorgeous Grey instead. One can but hope.

You probably think this sounds heartless. I'd have thought so myself at one time. I remember how it used to be when I was still an innocent, raised on Beatrix Potter. When I first met Doreen, she invited me to see her garden, which is as neat and pretty as she is, and I was admiring her perennials, when I noticed a fluffy tail bobbing about at the back of the border. "Nice lavender," I said, "fine phlox, cute squirrel."

The reaction was startling. Her body tensed, her eyes narrowed. "Squirrel?" she snarled. "Squirrel? The little..." and she started hurling invective and rocks at the border. My gentle new friend transformed into a fiend — by Squirrel

Nutkin? I was shocked and I told her so.

Now that I'm wiser in the ways of rodents, I called to tell her about my Blue Pearl disaster. I needed to let off steam and I could have used some sympathy. All I got was laughter, pretty callous laughter, I thought, and as she put the phone down I'm almost sure I caught the words, "I told you so." Next time the offspring of a thousand cutworms infest her petunias, she needn't come running to me for a shoulder to cry on!

As if this wasn't bad enough, I discovered that all but one of my snowdrops have been topped. So much for my dream carpet. Naturally I blamed the squirrels for this outrage too, until I noticed the remaining bud was delicately nibbled on one side. Slug damage. Now I suppose it's your turn to laugh. New Brunswick winters may be no joke but at least you don't have slugs in January. In the evening I caught seven of them in the act. One for each snowdrop stump. I was so mad I had no trouble stamping on them.

They were only small ones. It would take a stomach far stronger than mine to stamp on a banana slug. I usually pick up these giants on the tip of a trowel and hurl them across the road into the park, which is where I reckon they come from in the first place. Then I lie awake on rainy nights imagining them returning in waves and, in the morning, sure enough, there are often slime trails on the asphalt, which I'm darned sure are not heading *out* of the garden. In spite of their daunting appearance, the large native slugs are scavengers rather than aggressive herbivores and seem to do less damage in the garden than the smaller imports. A great point in their favour is that they help to keep the forest paths clean — which is more than many local dog owners do.

My attitude to slugs is changing. Even if I turned the whole garden into a fortress of copper fences, and a minefield of beer traps, and spent every night at work with my flashlight and fork, I'd still be fighting a losing battle. At best I'd create a brief slug vacuum into which would slide every neighbouring gastropod. (Gastropod means belly foot, so, like Napoleon's army, slugs march on their stomachs.) In the end, the only sensible way to cope is to concentrate on plants they dislike. They're surprisingly picky in their tastes. They'll shred the dwarf iris but shun the Japanese one. They're not keen on Japanese anemones either, or ornamental onions, Christmas roses, cranesbills and a host of other lovely plants, so a slug-safe garden needn't be a desert.

It would be a relief to call a truce because — this may be hard to believe — I think I may be developing a fondness for the slimy fellows/gals (they're hermaphrodite). It began when I watched the slugs last summer with Anne and my cousin. Until I saw their mating dance, I had no idea they were such unorthodox and fascinating creatures, and the more I learn about them, the less taste I have for wholesale carnage (snowdrop despoilers excepted).

This letter seems to be all sex and violence. I'll make myself a cup of tea, curl up by the fire with Thompson and Morgan's seed catalogue and try to be all sweetness and light next time.

Love, Elspeth

Kennebecasis River Road
Hampton, N.B.
February 21

DEAR ELSPETH,
A small girl brought your last letter right to our front door.
She said she'd found it in a ditch on her way home from
school and read our name on the sign outside the house. The
letter was wet and crumpled but readable. June is fine for
your visit. Any time is, actually. Though it does seem a long
way off.

It's lucky the squirrels climbing the trouser legs only get
sandwiches, I'd say. How old is Moses, anyway? He seemed
ancient when he lived in New Brunswick. I've not seen
coyotes here but Tina said she saw a coyote skirting the edge
of the marsh just the other day.

I don't know if you ever took part in it, but every year after
Christmas the firemen hold a tree-burning evening in the
park. They cook hot dogs and give out hot chocolate and
children slide down the hill on sleds and skate on the pond.
It seems to be one of the few events that brings the
community together. The environment group, of which I'm
secretary, asked if, instead of burning all the trees, we could
put some of them through a shredder. The organizers of the
evening reluctantly gave permission, on condition we kept
out of their way and left the place clean. A local businessman
donated his time and his shredder and the firemen said they
would let us have trees as they brought them in.

It wasn't too bad a day, cold and sunny; we started early in
the morning and shredded a few trees and then we waited.
The trees didn't seem forthcoming so I asked why we

couldn't have some from the huge pile near by. "Those are for burning," I was told. We shuffled our feet and stared covetously at the pile. Now and again a car drove up to deliver a tree. I wanted to rush out and ask, "Burn or mulch?" Hildegard's husband appeared and asked for a couple of bags of mulch. I thought poor old Hildegard was being done out of a job.

As the day wore on the firemen tossed more trees our way and watched us shred, bag and clean up. Coffee was made in the rescue truck and we were invited to help ourselves. I went into the truck, a vehicle only six months old and loaded with the latest equipment. One of the firemen gave me a tour and said that nowadays, because it was all so technical, the volunteers gave all their spare time to the department and had no time for other hobbies. I said, "The men probably enjoy the camaraderie." He looked at me as though I'd stumbled on some form of sexual perversion among the fire hoses. More and more men came for coffee and I was edged into the driving seat. I saw the key in the ignition and was tempted. "Mulcher Runs Off with Rescue Truck." I felt my foot on the accelerator, driving out of the park, lights flashing, whistles blowing with a load of prisoners. Instead, I slunk out and went back to the shredder.

In the end we collected one hundred and forty bags of mulch, which in this town of thirty-five hundred was difficult to get rid of. I offered mulch to one of the councillors; he threw up his hands in horror, as though he'd been offered bags of spent nuclear fuel rods. Not wanting to hang around any longer, we divided the remaining mulch between ourselves. So that's how I had eighteen bags to spread. In the next issue of the local paper was a long article about the event, written, I'm sure, by a pyromaniac. Nothing about the shredding.

Yesterday it rained and last night it froze, but today it's not bad. A mist is drifting over the marsh and wreathing Picwauket Mountain, and everyone's driveway is a sheet of ice. I was trying to scrape the path and saw that the creeping thyme was encased in a dome of ice, just like a preserved specimen. While I was scraping, the Leopard Couple ambled by. Mr. Leopard said he'd read in the paper that the daffodils and crocus were out in Vancouver.

"But did you know," I said, "that out there they have giant slugs — slugs as big as dogs, chomping away at the crocus and snowdrops. All you can hear is chomp, chomp, chomp."

"I don't care," Mrs. Leopard said. "I'd still like to live there." Mr. Leopard said it was as good as Vancouver here right now.

Since it was such a nice day, I took a stroll down the road. I talked to a neighbour trying to smash ice out of her driveway with a pickaxe. Leaning on her axe she told me she had just been on the phone to her brother in Vancouver and he said — you know of course what he said...

"But I bet he didn't tell you about the giant slugs they have out there that actually attack children," I said to her.

"Well, I'm sick of this," she said, giving the ice another bash with the axe.

"Out there," I said, "they have nothing to look forward to. Daffodils already. What'll they get in the spring?"

"What do we have to look forward to? More ice and snow and cold is all. And I'm sick of it," she said. She gave the ice such a whack it splintered through the air.

Love, Judy

231

Water Lane
West Vancouver, B.C.
March 4

DEAR JUDY,
I had a card this Christmas from friends who live near the southernmost tip of England. They were gloating that violets and jonquils were out already. This in the middle of December. I'm all for snowdrops in January but I don't approve of spring flowers blooming before Christmas. It gave me an idea though. Next time you feel sore about early flowering you-know-whats in you-know-where, you can tell yourself, and the Leopard Couple, that yours bloomed even earlier — as early as April of the previous year.

Kidnapping a truck full of firemen? Shame on you! And don't imagine I'd have bailed you out, though I doubt if they'd even have offered bail for such a crime. I need all my spare cash for the greenhouse fund.

Ray has started work on the courtyard. He's excavating under the deck to make a new storage area and has begun to build the stone wall which will form the greenhouse base.

I've been on Vancouver Island for a couple of days to visit Ellen. I wish you could have joined us for a Maritimers' reunion. We talked and dined around the clock but took time out to glance at the garden and check on her new rose which is also called Ellen. The deer are a problem, so Ellen-the-rose is in a fenced enclosure that used to be the vegetable plot. Either the deer haven't paid a visit recently, or they don't like snowdrops because outside the fence we found a couple of lovely colonies. Why do I have such a problem with snowdrops when everyone else seems to grow them without even trying? It's humbling.

I admired her chives, which were already well up, and she offered me some. She has plenty, even for a gourmet cook, so I was happy to split a clump and bring it home. They won't be used for anything fancy but I do love egg and chive sandwiches. She pickled her own herring this year, with delicious results. Although she told me how to do it, I don't think I'll be running out to meet the fishing fleet. It sounds messy. She buried the fish remains in the flower bed near her back door and the raccoons promptly disinterred them. Undaunted, she buried them again, put an old piece of carpet over the grave and weighted it down with rocks. It makes an interesting garden feature and it also makes me realise how much I like people whose places reflect their own tastes.

I do like to have bits of plants from other people's gardens. When we came out west I was determined to make a clean break and not pine for my old garden, so I brought nothing, not even a cutting. It made sense at the time but sometimes I regret it. I could at least have kept a piece of the little cranesbill Murray Hubbard gave me. It was *Geranium sanguineum var. striatum* but to me it was just Murray's geranium. I've since bought the same plant at a nursery, but it isn't really the same. It isn't *his*. And it doesn't have his enthusiasm for life either.

Not all gardeners are as charming and open-handed as Murray. I've met a few who are fiercely competitive. Most of us are covetous and generous in equal quantities, and the combination makes for lively free trade.

When Ray was back in New Brunswick, Sophie gave him a box full of the little hens-and-chicks she loves so well. I think

a few of the hens may have originated in my old greenhouse, where I started a batch from seeds. Eggs? I remember how surprised I was when they germinated without any trouble and turned into tough little succulents. It's lovely to have them here, nestling into cracks in the rock below the holly tree. I have to keep an eye on them because the holly berries find their way into the same cracks and if I didn't winkle them out I'd end up with a miniature holly forest.

I was so pleased to have Sophie's hens-and-chicks, I planted them in the best soil I could find, where of course they began to rot immediately. I knew perfectly well that they prefer a lean diet but I couldn't bear to think of them going hungry after such a long journey. To quote Sophie, "If stupidity bloomed, I'd be covered with flowers." Old Slovak saying.

It wasn't the first time, either, that I've almost killed hens-and-chicks by kindness. At the farm I planted several clumps with a generous spoonful of bone meal mixed into the soil under each. It wasn't the bone meal that did the damage, it was a skunk with a taste for phosphate. My flock was scattered far and wide but there's a happy ending to the story. Sort of. The rescued hens soon produced more chicks and the skunk also produced a fine batch of babies, no doubt with very healthy bones. The whole skunk family became regular visitors and ploughed up our lawn for us that summer.

The opponents of free trade point out that the plants which exchange hands most readily are the vigorous self-seeders, the rampant spreaders and the underground invaders. I've certainly welcomed disaster into my own garden on several occasions.

Hens and Chicks
Sempervivum tectorum

There was *Euphorbia cyparissias*. Its common name is spurge but it should be scourge. I planted it without a second thought, such a fresh and dainty-looking little thing it is. Three hundred and fifty years ago the great gardener Parkinson complained, "Spurge once planted will hardly be got rid of again." I wonder who gave it to him.

The common stonecrop, *Sedum acre*, was another gift. I started bits of it between paving stones at the farm, and a few years later our patio sank beneath a yellow tide. Pretty, but it left nowhere to sit. You'd think I'd have learned my lesson but I made the same kind of mistake here, planting a vigorous — too vigorous — little creeper, New Zealand burr, in my new cobblestone path.

The worst blunder I ever made was when I admired a neighbour's blue flowers and was told they were *Campanula rapunculoides*. I said I thought they were pretty and could he spare a bit? He seemed surprised and a little reluctant but finally handed over a few chunks which I dotted through the borders at the farm. This was how the Blue Devil claimed another victim. If you don't have *Campanula rapunculoides* in your garden yet — and I don't remember seeing it — don't ever be tempted! The roots are white and brittle and once you have them, you might as well hang up your hoe. Imagine a plate of noodles chopped up and stirred into your perennial bed, then imagine trying to pick out every fragment! Leave a single piece behind and a whole new generation of Blue Devils rises up to torment you. I never did get rid of them and I sometimes wonder if that's really why we moved out west.

If so, it was out of the frying pan into the variegated gout weed. This garden is thick with the stuff and it probably

arrived as a kindly donation, though I have seen it for sale
in garden centres, described as an attractive ground cover.
For anyone who wants their ground covered absolutely and
irrevocably — and yes, attractively in summer — I suppose
it's good stuff. I don't, so I dig it out by hand and leave the
area fallow for a year to make sure not a scrap remains.

I think the trick with horticultural exchanges is to give with
open hands but receive with open eyes.

The squirrel saga continues. Just when the cat litter
seemed to be working, just when I was thinking I could
patent the stuff as PP (pretty pungent) repellent, my source
dried up. Moses refused to deliver. I've tried pleading with
him. I've kept him indoors. I've made scratching noises in his
litter. I've turned on taps. All to no avail. Being Moses, he
would rather walk cross-legged than relinquish a drop of this
suddenly valuable commodity.

And talking of critters, as soon as I told you about my
growing interest in slugs, I discovered I was well behind the
times. A young friend presented me with a book of
Washington State slug recipes, which includes such amusing
delights as Slug Ravioli and Mock Escargots (slugs stuffed
into empty snail shells). Then I heard that an annual slugfest
is held near Vancouver, at Richmond Nature Park. After that
I came across a truly enormous grey slug on our own
driveway and thought I'd discovered a new species — until I
prodded it. A fake! A rubber slug! Could this be someone's
way of telling me I'm getting slugs on the brain? It couldn't
be you, so it had to be Jean and Charles. I'm trying to think
up a horrible revenge. Maybe I could put a fake robin in
their worm composter.

My flight is booked. May 18 to June 10. I'll stay with Kate

first but she starts a summer job in Halifax on June 1, so could you have me then?

Ellen sends her love and will write soon.

Elspeth

 Kennebecasis River Road
Hampton, N.B.
March 20

DEAR ELSPETH,
I envy you visiting Vancouver Island, especially today, as the wind is wild and the snow determined. I also envy you eating Ellen's cooking. Remember the Grand Manan pollack? And a rose called Ellen. Have you ever come across a plant called Elspeth? I know of none called Judy — only dogs. My mother told me I was named after a cow that belonged to a friend of hers, a lovely old creature she said. I was at a circus one time and heard the trainer yell at an elephant called Judy. Developers here call streets after members of their family, though I once went through a new development named after poets: Shelley Road, Keats Avenue and, not to be left out, Anon Street. But flowers make lovely names for girls. I knew twins called Cleome and Clarkia; unusual, but better than Lavatera.

We've had a deep freeze for the past few days and tons of snow. I was drinking my morning coffee and idly looking through the kitchen window. The snow beneath the flowering crab, awash with pink at Christmas, is now dotted with an extraordinary green, a pistachio green. The colour must be leaching from the sunflower seeds that we feed to the birds. But what a lovely colour. I was watching the birds trying to zero in on the feeder. They land on the ground, slide across the snow and are taken up by the wind into the air again. A few have sought shelter in the large footprints we've made in the snow, going to the feeder; seed has collected here and the goldfinches are gorging themselves.

Even though the weather has been bitter I don't seem to have felt as cold as previous years; I put this down to hot flashes — they must be good for something! Then my eighty-five-year old mother called from Wales and told me that she was going to cut the grass and that the *you know what* were all blooming. I can't get away from them!

After talking with my mother, instead of just watching the day slide by, I thought I'd better get something done. The *something* was to empty the compost container. So I get the container — it's only small — and a bag of spinach that has seen better days, and go and open the back door. Just outside I have a large bucket for compost, with a board across the top held in place with a couple of bricks. I lean out and as I try to pry the frozen board off the bucket, a gust of wind whips the bag of spinach out of my hand. Without thinking, I step outside and try to grab it and stand mesmerized as it spins around and around in the snow and whirls right over the fence. Suddenly, the door behind me slams. I'm shut out. I can't believe it. Every door locked. This is the first year we've ever had locks on the doors and I knew there was a reason why we shouldn't.

I'm wearing slippers and a sweater. I bang like a crazy

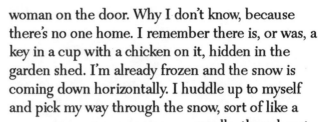

woman on the door. Why I don't know, because there's no one home. I remember there is, or was, a key in a cup with a chicken on it, hidden in the garden shed. I'm already frozen and the snow is coming down horizontally. I huddle up to myself and pick my way through the snow, sort of like a gazelle, though not as gracefully; the snow stings my face and blinds me. The shed door of course is frozen shut, so I throw myself against it. I'm tempted to break the windows but eventually, after many throws, which warm me up no end, I get inside. After a ground and air search I find the chicken cup and, lo and behold, the key; I was having grave doubts as to it still being in the shed at all. My slippers by now are sodden, and my feet so wet and cold I can hardly feel them. I wonder about frost-bite. Of course, now I can't shut the damned door so I leave it banging back and forth. On the way back up to the house I manage to tread in the same footprints, thinking all the time, What if I drop the key? By the time I get into the house I'm like an icicle. As Sophie said, "If stupidity bloomed…"

How lovely dry warm socks and another sweater felt, plus

the woodstove, though it took me ages to warm up. They say property is expensive in Vancouver. Pity.

Why ever did I think I was getting used to the cold? I must be mad.

I have found in life if you ever dare think you're getting ahead — bang! Crash! Something dumps on you. D'you find that? You must always be on your guard. Mind you, stacked against other disasters, being locked out on the tundra in a winter storm hardly bears mention. "Always be on your guard" sounds as though it should be on a coat of arms. Mine? My coat of arms would be a spade crossed with a garden fork with crabgrass rampant.

Talking about "rampant," I was given ground ivy — another one with pretty blue flowers — to cover a bank. They failed to tell me it would also cover house and garden. I like to get bits of plants from people because I'm reminded of them whenever I look at the plant.

Any chance of you bringing good weather?

Love, Judy

 Water Lane
West Vancouver, B.C.
April 1

DEAR JUDY,
Charles is keen on tulips and has pots and pots of them planted up on their balcony. I called this morning to warn them that the deadly Dutch tulip disease had broken out in

240

Vancouver and the only cure was to dip each bulb in a mixture of boiling vinegar and pickling spice.

There was a horrified silence on the line — until I told them to check their calendar. Aah, but revenge is sweet! I don't usually go in for this sort of thing but anyone who stoops to rubber slugs must expect the worst.

After that, they told me they were expecting a baby. Very funny!

BUT THEY ARE — no fooling! Jean is well and we're thrilled to bits. I can't wait to be a Granny. Poor mite; I'm already planning to teach it the botanical names of every plant in the garden. And speaking of names, I think you must have known about this when you mentioned flower names in your last letter. I like them too but wouldn't dare suggest them to the prospective parents who will no doubt have very decided ideas of their own.

There's a rhododendron called 'Elspeth' but I've never seen it. As far as I know there are no plants called Judy Maddocks but there is a rhododendron called 'Judy Spillane'. It's described as a late bloomer. Do you think this is significant?

I haven't noticed any ground ivy in this garden but I sometimes think I have every other noxious weed known to woman. As I'm sure I've told you already, the brambles are the worst. Until I came here I was fond of brambles. I still love blackberry and apple pie, and I admit that these West Coast brambles produce the biggest and sweetest fruit I've ever tasted, but they also produce the most aggressive stems, flinging them three, six metres in a season, over rocks and shrubs, swinging them, Tarzan-like, from trees and (I have the scars to prove it) wrapping them round the arms and ankles of anyone foolhardy enough to tangle with them.

Our bitter cress seems laughably harmless in comparison. It makes dainty rosettes of tiny leaves that pull up as easily as groundsel. They aren't fierce and they don't play leapfrog or sneak about underground. They procreate instead — efficiently and fast. Ripe seed pods explode at the slightest touch, firing seeds in all directions — hence the local name shot weed — and big plants can shoot right into your eyes if you're not careful. I don't know how many generations they squeeze into one year but it's several more than I can keep up with. Only daily vigilance defeats them and in the small areas I'm trying to keep clear, I pull them religiously, chanting *a shot weed in time saves nine thousand, nine hundred and ninety-nine*.

When we inherited a garden full of strange plants it didn't occur to me at first that we were also inheriting a collection of strange weeds. Getting to know their ways has been as interesting as getting to know the garden plants themselves.

The mail has just arrived with your package. What a treat to have my old friend the honeysuckle! It arrived in perfect condition and I potted it up immediately to keep it safe while I dither about where to plant it. Many thanks! Perhaps I should mention the generosity of gardeners in all my letters. Who knows what other goodies might come flying my way.

I received another great gift this week: snowdrops "in the green" and not just a couple of plants either. Shovelfuls! I didn't think I'd ever be so lucky. They came from a well-respected local gardener who scarcely knows me, so now I'm even more convinced that gardeners are an exceptionally kind-hearted lot.

Sunshine yesterday warmed up the soil and brought out that wonderful odour of damp earth. It also brought out the first rhododendron flowers and a few crocuses the squirrels missed, and of course it brought me out to gloat over all the brave new shoots and fuss over the lack of them. My seeds have arrived and I'm going to start some later today. It's early for some but the smell of spring makes me reckless — though not quite as drunkenly crazy as I used to feel after five months of winter in New Brunswick.

The weeping willow is a wash of lime green, like water colour painted on wet paper. The wild cherries next to it look more like an oil painting. They are speckled all over with opening buds and, against the darker shades of the cedars behind, look like an exercise in pointillism. Already the flower buds on the lilac are showing and the leaves are bigger than a mouse's ear, which means it's time to plant something. Unfortunately I forget what. Oak leaves are another indicator but I can't remember what they indicate either.

The earliest rhododendron to flower in this garden is Bo Peep. I'm a bit embarrassed by the name but at least she has one; she was wearing her label when we came. I still haven't identified many of the others. She grows in dreadfully dry soil under a pine tree in the jungle and I keep promising myself I'll rescue her and move her to a better spot, but haven't done so yet because all the better spots are occupied.

She is yellow, but an unobtrusive colour, barely more yellow than freshly opening leaves. In our first year, I didn't notice for some time that she was truly flowering, but when I did, I cut sprigs for the house and arranged them with the only other flowers I could find — both hellebores — the purple Lenten roses and the stinking hellebore (there really ought to be a better name). I would never have thought up

Stinking Hellebore
Helleborus foetidus

the combination but the pale greenish yellows of Bo Peep and the stinking hellebore with the dark, almost pewter coloured Lenten roses looked wonderful. They were the first flowers I picked from this garden and it's becoming a household tradition to arrange them together in a small pewter jug Ray bought in our student days.

The Lenten and the Christmas roses, like the oriental poppy, wilt when they're picked. The trick is to dip the tip of the stem in boiling water for a few seconds and then submerge the whole stem in tepid water for a few hours. Sometimes it works for me and sometimes it doesn't. You can also slit the stem down one side to help it soak up more water but I'm not sure this makes much difference. Strangely enough, the stinking hellebore stands up marvelously as a cut flower without any fuss at all.

Will it make it any easier for

you to read about my early season if I tell you that spring is advancing towards you up the east coast at a rate of twenty-five kilometres a day? It climbs mountains at a rate of thirty metres a day and, here on Vancouver's North Shore, which rises steeply from the sea, this means the uppermost gardens will have to wait ten more days before their star magnolias are as beautiful as mine is now. Had you noticed how I love to gloat?

Once the magnolia petals start to push off their fuzzy caps it doesn't take long for the whole tree to turn into a small snow storm. I know, you've had enough of snow storms, but this one is fragrant! For almost a month it really is the star of the garden.

It's one of the hardiest magnolias and it does survive in favoured spots in the Maritimes, though I wouldn't say it thrives. Have you ever seen one in New Brunswick? The buds are often damaged by frost, just as many camellia buds have been spoilt in Vancouver this year. Exposure to the morning sun is supposed to be especially damaging and it's probably true, though I've never seen the evidence with my own eyes.

I've grown sceptical about accepted horticultural wisdom. So much of it is, I suspect, passed blindly from book to book, mouth to mouth. *A clematis needs lime,* for instance. Does it really? And *Pruning cuts should be painted to keep out infection*. Not any more.

Pruning attracts misconceptions as readily as peonies attract ants. I'm sure you've read somewhere that spring flowering shrubs must be pruned immediately after flowering. True — if you must have your full quota of flowers the following year — but beginners think this means they'll kill the shrub if they prune at any other time, and of course that's nonsense.

I gave up putting a layer of crocks in the bottom of flower pots long ago. The plants seemed to get along just fine without it, but I felt a twinge of guilt every time I tipped soil into an uncrocked pot. It was reassuring to read, a few years ago, what I already knew — that crocks don't improve drainage after all.

I'm all for experimenting and questioning rules, at least in our own gardens where we can't harm anyone and a dead bush isn't the end of the world.

Love, Elspeth

P.S. A month from now, shall I really be sitting at your kitchen table, looking out at the new stone wall and the flowering crab apple? If we're lucky, it may even be warm enough to sit out in the secret place.

 Kennebecasis River Road
Hampton, N.B.
April 17

DEAR ELSPETH,
Congratulations on becoming a prospective grandmother. How d'you feel about sleeping with a grandfather?

I can't say that I've ever seen a star magnolia in the Maritimes, but what I have seen is another Camperdown. It was in the city and seemed a poor specimen compared to the one in Hampton. It was surrounded by buildings and didn't look at all happy, though has probably been there for years. I wonder if you've ever seen it? Though I don't think you were in love with Camperdowns when you lived here, were you?

At last I've been able to get out into the garden. There's a cloudless blue sky and no wind — chilly though, but I can at least do something outside if only for a short time. I decided to prune. Actually it's really just clipping things back, not proper pruning. I once saw an example of "cloud pruning" — cedar trees pruned to look like clouds. I thought they looked more like kidneys stuck on the end of sticks, about to be barbecued. Was this a poor example, d'you think? The shears slipped maybe.

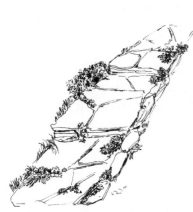

I wanted to clip the row of shrubs along the paved path I struggled to put down, the one that leads to the front door. I started with the weigela that has spent much of its life in the teeth of a gale and is such a toughy. Each summer it puts out a cascade of beautiful red blossoms. One day last summer the Leopard family passed by. Mrs. Leopard asked me its name.

"Well," she said, "I certainly don't want it in my garden."

"Why?" I asked.

"I don't like the way the branches flop down." They were overloaded with blossom and arching over. Fortunately the next week I had a garage sale and I don't know how many people admired it and asked me what it was called; it perked up no end. It's easy to propagate from cuttings. After the weigela I had a clip at the burning bush next to it; it's called a 'winged burning bush', a nice name, and an intense red in the fall. After the burning bush came a lilac that I'd transplanted from the large overgrown lilac hedge. I left it alone, but shaped up the cotoneaster next to it. Then the rose bush, a rugosa that was just about blocking the path. I clipped it right back; I have to keep my eye on it or it will be all over the path again.

All the shrubs along the path are constantly battered about; the wind comes up from the marsh and gathers strength in my garden. But I like to think they've helped form a small wind break for the perennial bed. So when you come you can admire the neatly clipped row.

I was clearing up after my activities when I noticed a woman strolling up the driveway. I saw no car and didn't recognize her so went down to meet her.

She said, "I was born in this house." She told me she was visiting her mother and was walking by so came in. We walked around the garden — nothing out, of course — and she told me she was a gardener. She looked at the tall cedars in the back and said that when she was growing up she could jump over them. Guess where she lives now — Vancouver Island of course. Soon, I feel, I shall be the only person living in New Brunswick.

While I was outside I heard a loud honking sound. Looking up, I saw a skein of Canada geese — the first I've seen this year. The ice is out of the river and the freshet is running; any day now the chimney swifts will return and then I will know that spring is here.

We are all looking forward to seeing you again, to see if West Coast living has changed you at all.

And don't forget, you'll need warm clothes!

Love, Judy

Water Lane
West Vancouver, B.C.
May 6

DEAR JUDY,
Generosity isn't the only trait common to gardeners. I laughed when I came across this extract from an autobiography of Colette. It's a letter from her mother, Sidonie, to Colette's husband.

> *Sir,*
> *You ask me to come and spend a week with you, which means I would be near my daughter, whom I adore. You who live with her know how rarely I see her, how much her presence delights me and I'm touched that you should ask me to come and see her. All the same, I'm not going to accept your kind invitation for the time being at any rate. The reason is that my pink cactus is probably going to flower…*

I've been facing a similar dilemma. The reason is that my blue poppies, planted last spring, are going to flower — at exactly the time I shall be away — and you, who know how much my daughter, my visit and my poppies mean to me will understand. All the same, I *am* going to accept your kind invitation. I have just been told that blue poppies have a quirky habit of dying if allowed to flower at their first attempt. Ordinarily I doubt if I'd have the strength of will to nip a blue poppy in the bud, but under the circumstances…

I suppose non-gardeners might think this kind of obsession

peculiar. But then, non-gardeners probably don't understand that real gardening is a passion. It may be slow and smouldering, it may have a quiet face, but, like any other passion, it has produced its share of havoc over the years. Monks have crashed from virtue — for a garden. Chinese Emperors have bankrupted the state — for a garden. Millionaires have drained their coffers to drain land — for a garden. And talking of passions, outside my window I'm thrilled to see that my Camperdown's tresses are healthy green with only a spattering of curly leaves. I haven't even bothered to pick off the aphids because the robins have nested again in the topknot of branches and I hate to disturb them. The dormant oil seems to be keeping the scale and hoppers at bay and miraculously the terrible gash has closed — a mere frost crack and unlikely to prove fatal.

The white narcissus are a great success. Mr. Dirr, in his *Manual of Woody Landscape Plants*, evaluated the landscape value of the American elm as *None anymore*, and he was right. The same goes for the Camperdown elm. It makes no sense to struggle with armies of pestilence when fine, trouble-free trees are available.

But Mr. Dirr was not in love.

This will be my last letter for some time. I don't think I ever told you how much your letters have meant to me since we moved — but I think you know.

I'll call from Kate's.

Gracious! I nearly forgot to tell you our news — Kimi and Rob are also expecting! Do you think the B.C. climate favours more than gardens, or is it just spring in the air?

How I've looked forward to finishing a letter with these words:

SEE YOU SOON!

With love as always, Elspeth